Karen

Karen

COMPLETE COOKERY

Chicken

DP
DEMPSEY
PARR

This is a Dempsey Parr Book
First printed in 2000

Dempsey Parr is an imprint of Parragon
Parragon
Queen Street House
4 Queen Street
Bath BA1 1HE, UK

ISBN: 1-84084-957-6

Printed in Italy

Note
Cup measurements in this book are for American cups.
Tablespoons are assumed to be 15 ml. Unless otherwise stated,
milk is assumed to be whole, eggs are large,
and pepper is freshly ground black pepper.

Contents

Introduction   4

Soups & Appetizers   8

Quick Dishes   80

Roasts & Casseroles   152

Barbecues & Broils   236

Dinner Party Dishes   296

Index   384

Introduction

One of the easiest and least disruptive ways to reduce your fat intake is to change the way you cook. Trying new recipes, even with familiar ingredients, is fun and will result in the pleasure of eating delicious meals that are also healthier.

Chicken has become justly popular around the world and plays an important part in the modern diet, being reasonably priced and nutritionally sound. A versatile meat, it lends itself to an enormous range of cooking methods and cuisines. Its unassertive flavor means that it is equally suited to cooking with both sweet and savory flavors. Because it has a low fat content, especially without the skin, it is an ideal meat for low cholesterol and calorie-controlled diets. As well as being an excellent source of protein, chicken contains valuable minerals, such as potassium and phosphorus, and some of the B vitamins.

Cooking Methods:

Roasting Remove any fat from the body cavity. Rinse the bird inside and out with water, then pat dry with paper towels. Season the cavity generously with salt and pepper and add stuffing, herbs or lemon if wished. Spread the breast of the chicken with softened butter or oil. Set on a rack in a roasting pan or shallow baking dish. Roast the bird, basting two or three times with the pan juices during roasting. If the chicken is browning too quickly, cover it with foil. Test for doneness by using a meat thermometer or insert a skewer into the thickest part of the thigh. If the chicken is cooked, the juices will run clear with no trace of pink. Put the bird on a carving board and leave to rest for 15 minutes before serving. Make a sauce or otherwise a gravy from the juices left in the roasting pan.

Broiling

The intense heat of the broiler quickly seals the succulent flesh beneath a crisp, golden exterior. Place the chicken 4–6 inches away from a medium heat source. If the chicken seems to be browning too quickly, reduce the heat slightly. If the chicken is broiled at too high a temperature too near to the heat, the outside will burn before the inside is cooked. If it is cooked for too long under a low heat, it will dry out. Divide the chicken into joints to ensure even cooking. Breast meat, if cooked in one piece, can be rather dry, so it is best to cut it into chunks for kabobs. Wings are best for speedy broiling.

Frying is suitable for small thighs, drumsticks, and joints. Dry the chicken pieces with paper towels so that they brown properly and to prevent spitting during cooking. The chicken can be coated in seasoned flour, egg and bread crumbs, or a batter. Heat oil or a mixture of oil and butter in a heavy skillet. When the oil is very hot, add the chicken pieces, skin-side down. Fry until deep golden brown all over, turning the pieces frequently during cooking. Drain well on paper towels before serving.

Sautéeing is ideal for small pieces or small birds such as baby chickens. Heat a little oil or a mixture of oil and butter in a heavy skillet. Add the chicken and fry over a medium heat until golden brown, turning frequently. Add stock or other liquid, bring to the boil, then cover, and reduce the heat. Cook gently until the chicken is cooked through.

Stir-Frying is good when skinless, boneless chicken is cut into small pieces of equal size to ensure that the meat cooks evenly and stays succulent. Preheat a wok or saucepan before adding a small amount of oil. When the oil starts to smoke, add the chicken and stir-fry with your chosen flavorings for 3–4 minutes until cooked through. Other ingredients can be cooked at the same time, or the chicken can be cooked by itself, then removed from the pan while you stir-fry the remaining ingredients. Return the chicken to the pan once the other ingredients are cooked.

Casseroling is a good method for cooking joints from larger, more mature chickens, although smaller chickens can be cooked whole. The slow cooking produces tender meat with a good flavor. Brown the chicken in butter or oil or a mixture of both. Add some stock, wine, or a mixture of both, with seasonings and herbs, cover, and cook on top of the stove or in the oven until the chicken is tender. Add a selection of lightly sautéed vegetables about halfway through the cooking time.

Braising is a method which does not require liquid. The chicken pieces or a small whole chicken and vegetables are cooked together slowly in a low oven. Heat some oil in an ovenproof, flameproof casserole and gently fry the chicken until golden. Remove the chicken and fry a selection of vegetables until they are almost tender. Replace the chicken, cover

tightly and cook very gently on the top of the cooker or in a low oven until the chicken and vegetables are tender.

Poaching is a gentle cooking method that produces tender chicken and a stock that can be used to make a sauce to serve with the chicken. Put a whole chicken, a bouquet garni, a leek, a carrot, and an onion in a large flameproof casserole. Cover with water, season, and bring to the boil. Simmer for 1½–2 hours until the chicken is tender. Lift the chicken out, discard the bouquet garni, and use the stock to make a sauce. Blend the vegetables to thicken the stock and serve with the chicken.

Food Safety & Tips

Chicken is liable to be contaminated by salmonella bacteria, which can cause severe food poisoning. When storing, handling, and preparing poultry, certain precautions must be observed to prevent the possibility of food poisoning.

• Check the sell-by date and best before date. After buying, take the chicken home quickly, preferably in a freezer bag or cool box.

• Return frozen birds immediately to the freezer.

• If storing in the refrigerator, remove the wrappings and store any giblets separately. Place the chicken in a shallow dish to catch drips. Cover loosely with foil and store on the bottom shelf of the refrigerator for no more than two or three days, depending on the best-before date. Avoid any contact between raw chicken and cooked food during storage and preparation. Wash your hands thoroughly after handling raw chicken.

• Prepare raw chicken on a chopping board that can be easily cleaned and bleached, such as a non-porous, plastic board.

• Frozen birds should be defrosted before cooking. If time permits, defrost for about 36 hours in the refrigerator, or thaw for about 12 hours in a cool place. Bacteria breed in warm food at room temperature and when chicken is thawing. Cooking at high temperatures kills bacteria. There should be no ice crystals and the flesh should feel soft and flexible. Cook the chicken as soon as possible after thawing.

• Make sure that chicken is cooked. Test for doneness using a meat thermometer – the thigh should reach at least 175°F when cooked – or pierce the thickest part of a thigh with a skewer, the juices should run clear, not pink or red. Never partially cook chicken with the intention of completing cooking later.

Soups & Appetizers

Chicken soup has a long tradition of being comforting and good for us and some cultures even think of it as a cure for all ills. It is certainly satisfying, full of flavor, and easy to digest. For the best results, use a good homemade chicken stock, although when time is at a premium, a good quality bouillon cube can be used instead. Every cuisine in the world has its own favorite version of chicken soup and in this section you'll find a selection of recipes from as far afield as Italy, Scotland, and China.

As chicken is so versatile and quick to cook, it is perfect for innovative and appetizing snacks. Its unassertive flavor means that it can be enlivened by exotic fruits and spices and oriental ingredients, such as mirin, sesame oil, and fresh gingerroot. There are fritters, salads, and drumsticks that are stuffed and baked, or served with delicious fruity salsas. Because chicken pieces travel well and are easy to eat, many of the recipes are ideal to take on picnics or to pack into a lunch box.

Cream of Chicken Soup

Tarragon adds a delicate aniseed flavor to this tasty soup.
If you can't find tarragon, use parsley for a fresh taste.

Serves 4

INGREDIENTS

4 tbsp unsalted butter
1 large onion, peeled and chopped
10^1/$_2$ oz cooked chicken,
   shredded finely
2^1/$_2$ cups chicken stock
1 tbsp chopped fresh tarragon

^{2}/$_3$ cup heavy cream
salt and pepper
fresh tarragon leaves, to garnish
deep fried croutons, to serve

1 Melt the butter in a large saucepan and fry the onion for 3 minutes.

2 Add the chicken to the pan with 1¼ cups of the chicken stock.

3 Bring to the boil and simmer for 20 minutes. Allow to cool, then liquidize the soup.

4 Add the remainder of the stock and season with salt and pepper.

5 Add the chopped tarragon, pour the soup into a tureen or individual serving bowls, and add a swirl of cream.

6 Garnish the soup with fresh tarragon and serve with deep fried croutons.

VARIATION

To make garlic croutons, crush 3–4 garlic cloves in a pestle and mortar and add to the oil.

VARIATION

If you can't find fresh tarragon, freeze-dried tarragon makes a good substitute. Light cream can be used instead of the heavy cream.

Cream of Chicken & Lemon Soup

*This refreshing soup with its refreshing lemon flavor
is perfect on summer days.*

Serves 4

INGREDIENTS

4 tbsp butter
8 shallots, sliced thinly
2 medium carrots, sliced thinly
2 celery stalks, sliced thinly
9 oz skinless chicken breast meat,
   chopped finely

3 lemons
5 cups chicken stock
$^2/_3$ cup heavy cream
salt and pepper

sprigs of parsley and lemon slices,
   to garnish

1 Melt the butter in a large saucepan, add the vegetables and chicken, and cook gently for 8 minutes.

2 Thinly pare the lemons and blanch the lemon rind in boiling water for 3 minutes.

3 Squeeze the juice from the lemons.

4 Add the lemon rind and freshly squeezed lemon juice to the pan with the chicken stock.

5 Bring slowly to a boil and simmer for about 50 minutes. Leave the soup to cool then transfer to a food processor and blend until smooth. Return the soup to the saucepan, reheat, season with salt and pepper to taste, and add the heavy cream. Do not boil at this stage or the soup will curdle.

6 Transfer the soup to a tureen or warm individual bowls. Serve, garnished with parsley and lemon slices.

VARIATION

*For an alternative citrus flavor,
use 4 oranges in place of the
lemons. The recipe can also
be adapted to make duck
and orange soup.*

Cream of Chicken & Orange Soup

*For a tangy flavor, lemons can be used instead of oranges and the recipe
can be adapted to make duck and orange soup.*

Serves 4

INGREDIENTS

4 tbsp butter
8 shallots, sliced thinly
2 medium carrots, sliced thinly
2 stalks celery, sliced thinly

8 oz skinless chicken breast, chopped
  finely
3 oranges
5 cups chicken stock
1/3 cup heavy cream
salt and white pepper

sprig of parsley and 3 orange slices,
  to garnish

1   Melt the butter in a large saucepan, add the shallots, carrot, celery, and chicken meat and cook gently for 8 minutes, stirring occasionally.

2   Using a potato peeler or sharp knife, thinly pare the oranges and blanch the rind in boiling water for about 3 minutes.

3   Squeeze the juice from the oranges. Add the orange rind and orange juice to the pan together with the chicken stock.

4   Bring slowly to a boil and simmer for 50 minutes. Cool the soup, then liquidize in a blender or food processor until smooth.

5   Return the soup to the saucepan, reheat, season to taste, and add the cream. Do not boil at this stage or the soup will curdle.

6   Transfer the soup to a serving dish or individual bowls. Garnish with a sprig of parsley and orange slices and serve with soda bread.

VARIATION

*Use 2 small lemons
in place of the oranges. Look for
organic or unwaxed lemons when
using peel.*

Cream of Chicken & Tomato Soup

*This soup is very good made with fresh tomatoes,
but if you prefer, you can use canned tomatoes.*

Serves 2

INGREDIENTS

4 tbsp unsalted butter
1 large onion, chopped
1 lb 2 oz chicken,
   shredded very finely
$2^1/_2$ cups chicken stock
6 medium tomatoes, chopped finely

pinch of bicarbonate of baking soda
1 tbsp superfine sugar
$^2/_3$ cup heavy cream
salt and pepper
fresh basil leaves, to garnish
croutons, to serve

1 Melt the butter in a large
saucepan and fry the onion
and shredded chicken for
5 minutes.

2 Add $1^1/_4$ cups chicken stock
to the pan, with the tomatoes
and bicarbonate of baking soda.

3 Bring the soup to a boil and
simmer for 20 minutes.

4 Allow the soup to cool, then
blend in a food processor.

5 Add the remaining chicken
stock, season with salt and
pepper, then add the sugar. Pour
the soup into a tureen and add a
swirl of heavy cream. Serve the
soup with croutons and garnish
with fresh basil leaves.

COOK'S TIP

*For a healthier version of this soup,
use light cream instead
of the heavy cream
and omit the sugar.*

VARIATION

*For an Italian-style soup, add
1 tbsp chopped fresh basil with the
stock in step 2. Alternatively, add
$^1/_2$ tsp curry powder or chilli
powder to make a spicier
version of this soup.*

Cream of Lemon & Chicken Soup with Spaghetti

This delicately flavored summer soup is surprisingly easy to make.

Serves 4

INGREDIENTS

4 tbsp butter
8 shallots, thinly sliced
2 carrots, thinly sliced
2 celery stalks, thinly sliced
8 oz boned chicken breasts, finely chopped

3 lemons
5 cups chicken stock
8 oz dried spaghetti, broken into small pieces
$5/8$ cup heavy cream
salt and white pepper

TO GARNISH:
fresh parsley sprig
3 lemon slices, halved

1 Melt the butter in a large saucepan. Add the shallots, carrots, celery, and chicken and cook over a low heat, stirring occasionally, for 8 minutes.

2 Thinly pare the lemons and blanch the lemon peel in boiling water for 3 minutes. Squeeze the juice from the lemons.

3 Add the lemon peel and juice to the pan, together with the chicken stock. Bring slowly to a boil over a low heat and simmer for 40 minutes.

4 Add the spaghetti to the pan and cook for 15 minutes. Season to taste with salt and white pepper and add the cream. Heat through, but do not allow the soup to boil or it will curdle.

5 Pour the soup into a tureen or individual bowls, garnish with the parsley and half slices of lemon, and serve immediately.

COOK'S TIP

You can prepare this soup up to the end of step 3 in advance, so that all you need do before serving is heat it through before adding the pasta and the finishing touches.

Chicken Mulligatawny Soup

*This spicy soup was brought to the west by army
and service personnel returning from India.*

Serves 4

INGREDIENTS

4 tbsp butter
1 onion, sliced
1 garlic clove, minced
1 lb 2 oz chicken, diced
$^{1}/_{3}$ cup smoked rindless
    bacon, diced
1 small turnip, diced
2 carrots, diced

1 small cooking apple, diced
2 tbsp mild curry powder
1 tbsp curry paste
1 tbsp tomato paste
1 tbsp all-purpose flour
5 cups chicken stock
$^{2}/_{3}$ cup heavy cream
salt and pepper

1 tsp of chopped fresh
    cilantro, to garnish

1 Melt the butter in a large
saucepan and cook the onion,
garlic, chicken, and bacon for
5 minutes.

2 Add the turnip, carrots, and
apple and cook for a further
two minutes.

3 Blend in the curry powder,
curry paste, and tomato paste,
and sprinkle over the all-purpose
flour.

4 Add the chicken stock and
bring to a boil, cover, and
simmer over a gentle heat for
about 1 hour.

5 Liquidize the soup. Reheat,
season well with salt and
pepper to taste and gradually blend
in the heavy cream. Garnish the
soup with chopped fresh cilantro
and serve over small bowls of
boiled or fried rice.

COOK'S TIP

*This soup may be frozen for
up to 1 month; if stored for any
longer, the spices may cause
it to taste musty.*

Chicken, Guinea Fowl, & Spaghetti Soup

Guinea fowl has a similar texture to chicken, and although it has a milder flavor than other game, it has a slightly gamier flavor than chicken.

Serves 6

INGREDIENTS

1 lb 2 oz skinless chicken, chopped
1 lb 2 oz skinless guinea
    fowl meat
2 1/2 cups chicken stock
1 small onion
6 peppercorns

1 tsp cloves
pinch of mace
2/3 cup heavy cream
2 tsp butter
2 tsp all-purpose flour

1 cup quick-cook spaghetti, broken
    into short pieces and cooked
2 tbsp chopped fresh parsley,
    to garnish

1 Put the chicken and guinea fowl meat into a large saucepan with the chicken stock.

2 Bring to a boil and add the onion, peppercorns, cloves, and mace. Simmer gently for about 2 hours until the stock is reduced by one-third.

3 Strain the soup, skim off any fat, and remove any bones from the chicken and guinea fowl.

4 Return the soup and meat to a clean saucepan. Add the heavy cream and bring to a boil slowly.

5 To make a roux, melt the butter and stir in the flour until it has a paste-like consistency. Add to the soup, stirring until slightly thickened.

6 Just before serving, add the cooked quick-cook spaghetti.

7 Transfer the soup to individual serving bowls, garnish with parsley and serve.

VARIATION

Instead of spaghetti, use small pasta shapes such as ziti or macaroni.

Chicken & Pea Soup

A hearty soup that is so simple to make yet packed with flavor.
You can use either whole green peas or green or yellow split peas.

Serves 4–6

INGREDIENTS

3 smoked, streaky, rindless bacon
  slices, chopped
2 lb chicken, chopped
1 large onion, chopped
1 tbsp butter
$2^{1}/_{2}$ cups ready-soaked peas
10 cups chicken stock

$^{2}/_{3}$ cup heavy cream
2 tbsp chopped fresh parsley

salt and pepper
cheesy croûtes, to garnish

1 Put the bacon, chicken, and onion into a large saucepan with a little butter and cook over a gentle heat for 8 minutes.

2 Add the peas and the stock to the pan, bring to a boil, season lightly with salt and pepper, cover and simmer for 2 hours.

3 Blend the heavy cream into the soup, sprinkle with parsley, and top with cheesy croûtes (see Cook's Tip, right).

COOK'S TIP

Croûtes are slices of French bread that are fried or baked, then they can be sprinkled with grated cheese and lightly toasted.

VARIATION

Use $3^{1}/_{2}$ oz chopped ham instead of the bacon, if you prefer.

COOK'S TIP

If using dried peas, soak them for several hours or overnight in a large bowl of cold water. Alternatively, bring them to a boil in a pan of cold water. Remove from the heat and leave to cool in the water. Drain and rinse the beans before adding them to the soup.

Tom's Chicken Soup

The potato has been part of the Irish diet for centuries. This recipe is originally from the north of Ireland, in the beautiful area of Moira, County Down.

Serves 4

INGREDIENTS

3 smoked, streaky,
rindless bacon slices, chopped
1 lb 2 oz boneless chicken, chopped
2 tbsp butter
3 medium potatoes, chopped
3 medium onions, chopped

$2^{1}/_{2}$ cups giblet or chicken stock
$2^{1}/_{2}$ cups milk
$^{2}/_{3}$ cup heavy cream
salt and pepper
2 tbsp chopped fresh parsley
soda bread, to serve

1 Gently fry the bacon and chicken in a large saucepan for 10 minutes.

2 Add the butter, potatoes, and onions and cook for 15 minutes, stirring all the time.

3 Add the stock and milk, then bring the soup to a boil, and simmer for 45 minutes. Season with salt and pepper to taste.

4 Blend in the cream and simmer for 5 minutes. Stir in the chopped fresh parsley, transfer the soup to a warm tureen or individual bowls, and serve with Irish soda bread.

COOK'S TIP

Soda bread is not made with yeast as bread usually is. Instead it is made with baking soda as the rising agent. It can be made with all-purpose or whole-wheat flour.

VARIATION

For a more filling, main course soup, you can add any number of different vegetables, for example leeks, celery root, or corn.

Garbanzo Bean & Chicken Soup

This hearty and nourishing soup is an ideal appetizer for a family supper.

Serves 4

INGREDIENTS

2 tbsp butter
3 scallions, chopped
2 garlic cloves, minced
1 fresh marjoram sprig,
  finely chopped

12 oz boned chicken
  breasts, diced
12 oz can garbanzo beans, drained
5 cups chicken stock
1 bouquet garni
1 red bell pepper, diced

1 green bell pepper, diced

1 cup small dried pasta shapes, such
  as macaroni
salt and white pepper
croutons, to serve

1 Melt the butter in a large saucepan. Add the scallions, garlic, sprig of fresh marjoram, and the diced chicken, and cook, stirring frequently, over a medium heat for 5 minutes.

2 Add the chicken stock, garbanzo beans, and bouquet garni to the pan and season to taste with salt and white pepper.

3 Bring the soup to a boil, lower the heat, and simmer gently for about 2 hours.

4 Add the diced bell peppers and pasta to the pan, then simmer for a further 20 minutes.

5 Transfer the soup to a warm tureen. To serve, ladle the soup into individual serving bowls and serve immediately, garnished with the croutons.

COOK'S TIP

If you prefer, you can use dried garbanzo beans. Cover with cold water and set aside to soak for 5–8 hours. Drain and add the beans to the soup, according to the recipe, and allow an additional 30 minutes–1 hour cooking time.

Chicken & Corn Soup

This heart-warming soup is both quick and easy to make.

Serves 4

INGREDIENTS

1 lb boned chicken breasts, cut into strips	1 tbsp cornstarch
	3 tbsp milk
5 cups chicken stock	
5/8 cup heavy cream	6 oz corn-on-the-cob kernels
3/4 cup dried vermicelli	salt and pepper

1 Put the chicken, stock, and cream into a large saucepan and bring to a boil over a low heat. Reduce the heat slightly and simmer for about 20 minutes. Season the soup with salt and black pepper to taste.

2 Meanwhile, cook the vermicelli in lightly salted boiling water for 10-12 minutes, until just tender. Drain the pasta and keep warm.

3 In a small bowl, mix together the cornstarch and milk to make a smooth paste. Stir the cornstarch into the soup until thickened.

4 Add the corn-on-the-cob and vermicelli to the pan and heat through.

5 Transfer the soup to a warm tureen or individual soup bowls and serve immediately.

COOK'S TIP

If you are short of time, buy ready-cooked chicken, remove any skin, and cut it into slices.

VARIATION

For crab and corn soup, substitute 1 lb cooked crabmeat for the chicken breasts. Flake the crabmeat well before adding it to the saucepan and reduce the cooking time by 10 minutes. For a Chinese-style soup, substitute egg noodles for the vermicelli and use canned, creamed corn-on-the-cob.

Chicken Consommé

This is a very flavorful soup, especially if you make it from real chicken stock. Egg shells are used to give a crystal-clear appearance.

Serves 8–10

INGREDIENTS

8 cups chicken stock
$^2/_3$ cup medium sherry
4 egg whites plus egg shells

4 oz cooked chicken, sliced thinly
salt and pepper

1 Place the chicken stock and sherry in a large saucepan and heat gently for 5 minutes.

2 Add the egg whites and the egg shells to the chicken stock and whisk until the mixture begins to boil.

3 Remove the pan from the heat and allow the mixture to subside for 10 minutes. Repeat this process three times. This allows the egg white to trap the sediments in the chicken stock to clarify the soup. Let the consommé cool for 5 minutes.

4 Carefully place a piece of fine cheesecloth over a saucepan. Ladle the soup over the muslin and strain into the saucepan.

5 Repeat this process twice, then gently re-heat the consommé. Season with salt and pepper to taste and add the cooked chicken slices. Pour the soup into a warm serving dish or individual bowls.

6 Garnish the consommé with any of the suggestions in the Cook's Tip, right.

COOK'S TIP

Consommé is usually garnished with freshly cooked pasta shapes, noodles, rice, or lightly cooked vegetables. Alternatively, you could garnish it with omelet strips, drained first on paper towels.

Chicken & Leek Soup

This satisfying soup can be served as a main course.
You can add rice and bell peppers to make it even more hearty, as well as colorful.

Serves 6

INGREDIENTS

12 oz boneless chicken
12 oz leeks
2 tbsp butter
5 cups chicken stock

1 bouquet garni sachet
8 pitted prunes, halved
salt and white pepper

cooked rice and diced bell peppers
(optional)

1 Using a sharp knife, cut the chicken and leeks into 1-inch pieces.

2 Melt the butter in a large saucepan, add the chicken and leeks, and fry for 8 minutes, stirring occasionally.

3 Add the chicken stock and bouquet garni sachet to the mixture in the pan, and season with salt and pepper to taste.

4 Bring the soup to a boil and simmer over a gentle heat for 45 minutes.

5 Add the pitted prunes with some cooked rice and diced bell peppers (if using), and simmer for 20 minutes. Remove the bouquet garni sachet and discard. Pour the soup into a warm tureen or individual bowls and serve.

COOK'S TIP

If you have time, make the chicken stock yourself. Alternatively, you can buy good fresh stock from supermarkets.

COOK'S TIP

Instead of the bouquet garni sachet, you can use a bunch of fresh, mixed herbs, tied together with string. Choose herbs such as parsley, thyme, and rosemary.

Chicken Soup with Cilantro Dumplings

Use the strained vegetables and chicken to make little patties. Simply mash with a little butter, shape them into round cakes, and fry in butter or oil until golden brown.

Serves 6-8

INGREDIENTS

2 lb chicken meat, sliced
$1/2$ cup all-purpose flour
$1/2$ cup butter
3 tbsp sunflower oil
1 large carrot, chopped
1 stalk celery, chopped
1 onion, chopped
1 small turnip, chopped
$1/2$ cup sherry

1 tsp thyme
1 bay leaf
8 cups chicken stock
salt and pepper
crusty bread, to serve

DUMPLINGS:
$1/2$ cup self-rising flour
1 cup fresh bread crumbs
2 tbsp shredded suet
2 tbsp chopped fresh cilantro
2 tbsp finely grated lemon peel
1 egg
salt and pepper

1 Coat the chicken pieces with the flour and season.

2 Melt the butter in a saucepan and fry the chicken pieces until they are lightly browned.

3 Add the oil to the pan and brown the vegetables. Add the sherry and the remaining ingredients except the stock.

4 Cook for 10 minutes, then add the stock. Simmer for 3 hours, strain into a clean saucepan, and allow to cool.

5 To make the dumplings, mix together all the dry ingredients in a large clean bowl. Add the egg and blend in thoroughly then add enough milk to make a moist dough.

6 Shape into small balls and roll them in a little flour.

7 Cook the dumplings in boiling salted water for 10 minutes.

8 Remove them carefully with a draining spoon and add them to the soup. Cook for a further 12 minutes, then serve.

Chicken Wonton Soup

*This Chinese-style soup is delicious as an appetizer
to an oriental meal or as a light meal.*

Serves 4-6

INGREDIENTS

FILLING:

12 oz ground chicken

1 tbsp soy sauce

1 tsp grated, fresh gingerroot

1 garlic clove, minced

2 tsp sherry

2 scallions, chopped

1 tsp sesame oil

1 egg white

$1/2$ tsp cornstarch

$1/2$ tsp sugar

about 35 wonton skins

SOUP:

6 cups chicken stock

1 tbsp light soy sauce

1 scallion, shredded

1 small carrot, cut into
very thin slices

1 Combine all the ingredients for the filling and mix well.

2 Place a small spoonful of the filling in the center of each wonton skin.

3 Dampen the edges and gather up the wonton skin to form a pouch enclosing the filling.

4 Cook the filled wontons in boiling water for 1 minute or until they float to the top.

5 Remove with a draining spoon. Bring the chicken stock to a boil.

6 Add the soy sauce, scallion, carrot, and wontons to the soup. Simmer gently for 2 minutes then serve.

VARIATION

*Substitute the chicken for
ground pork.*

COOK'S TIP

*Look for wonton skins in Chinese
or oriental supermarkets. Fresh
skins can be found in the chilled
compartment and they can be
frozen if you wish. Wrap
in plastic wrap before freezing.*

Chicken & Asparagus Soup

*This light, clear soup has a delicate flavor of asparagus
and herbs. Use a good quality stock for best results.*

Serves 4

INGREDIENTS

8 oz fresh asparagus
3³/₄ cups fresh chicken stock
²/₃ cup dry white wine

1 sprig each fresh parsley, dill
   and tarragon
1 garlic clove
¹/₃ cup vermicelli rice noodles

12 oz lean cooked chicken, finely
   shredded
salt and white pepper
1 small leek, shredded, to garnish

1 Wash the asparagus and trim away the woody ends. Cut each spear into pieces 1½ inches long.

2 Pour the stock and wine into a large saucepan and bring to a boil.

3 Wash the herbs and tie them with clean string. Peel the garlic clove and add, with the herbs, to the saucepan together with the asparagus and noodles. Cover and simmer for 5 minutes.

4 Stir in the chicken and plenty of seasoning. Simmer gently for a further 3-4 minutes until heated through.

5 Trim the leek, slice it down the center, and wash under running water to remove any dirt. Shake dry and shred finely.

6 Remove the herbs and garlic from the pan and discard. Ladle the soup into warm bowls, sprinkle with shredded leek and serve at once.

VARIATION

You can use any of your favorite herbs in this recipe, but choose those with a subtle flavor so that they do not overpower the asparagus. Small, tender asparagus spears give the best results and flavor.

COOK'S TIP

Rice noodles contain no fat and are an ideal substitute for egg noodles.

Chicken & Pasta Broth

This satisfying soup makes a good lunch or supper dish and you can use any vegetables that you have at hand. Children will love the tiny pasta shapes.

Serves 6

INGREDIENTS

12 oz boneless
   chicken breasts
2 tbsp sunflower oil
1 medium onion, diced
1^1/$_2$ cups carrots, diced
9 oz cauliflower flowerets

3^3/$_4$ cups chicken stock
2 tsp dried mixed herbs
4^1/$_2$ oz small pasta shapes
salt and pepper

Parmesan cheese (optional)
   and crusty bread, to serve

1 Using a sharp knife, finely dice the chicken, discarding any skin.

2 Heat the oil in a large saucepan and quickly sauté the chicken and vegetables until they are lightly colored.

3 Stir in the stock and herbs. Bring to a boil and add the pasta shapes. Return to a boil, cover, and simmer for 10 minutes, stirring occasionally to prevent the pasta shapes sticking together.

4 Season with salt and pepper to taste and sprinkle with Parmesan cheese, if using. Serve with fresh crusty bread.

COOK'S TIP

You can use any small pasta shapes for this soup – try conchigliette or ditalini or even spaghetti broken up into small pieces. To make a fun soup for children, add animal-shaped or alphabet pasta.

VARIATION

Broccoli flowerets can be used to replace the cauliflower flowerets. Substitute 2 tablespoons chopped fresh mixed herbs for the dried mixed herbs.

Thai Chicken Noodle Soup

Quick to make, this hot and spicy soup is hearty and warming. If you like your food really fiery, add a chopped dried or fresh chili with its seeds.

Serves 4

INGREDIENTS

1 sheet of dried egg noodles
  from a 9 oz pack
1 tbsp oil
4 skinless, boneless
  chicken thighs, diced
1 bunch scallions, sliced
2 garlic cloves, chopped

$^3/_4$ inch piece fresh
  gingerroot, finely chopped
$3^3/_4$ cups chicken stock
scant 1 cup coconut milk
3 tsp red Thai curry paste
3 tbsp peanut butter
2 tbsp light soy sauce

1 small red bell pepper,
  chopped
$^1/_2$ cup frozen peas
salt and pepper

1 Put the noodles in a shallow dish and soak in boiling water following the instructions on the packet.

2 Heat the oil in a large saucepan or wok, add the chicken, and fry for 5 minutes, stirring until lightly browned. Add the white part of the spring onions (scallions), the garlic and ginger and fry for 2 minutes, stirring. Add the stock, coconut milk, curry paste, peanut butter and soy sauce. Season with salt and pepper to taste. Bring to a boil, stirring, then simmer for 8 minutes, stirring occasionally. Add the red bell pepper, peas, and green scallion tops and cook for 2 minutes.

3 Add the drained noodles and heat through. Spoon into individual bowls and serve with a spoon and fork.

VARIATION

Green Thai curry paste can be used instead of red curry paste for a less fiery flavor.

Dickensian Chicken Broth

This soup is made with traditional Scottish ingredients. It should be left for at least two days before being re-heated, then served with oatmeal cakes or bread.

Serves 4

INGREDIENTS

$^1/_3$ cup pre-soaked dried peas
2 lb diced chicken, fat removed
5 cups chicken stock
$2^1/_2$ cups water
$^1/_4$ cup barley

1 large carrot, peeled and diced
1 small turnip, peeled and diced
1 large leek, thinly sliced
1 red onion, chopped finely
salt and white pepper

1 Put the peas and chicken into a pan, add the stock, and water and bring slowly to a boil.

2 Skim the stock as it boils using a draining spoon.

3 When all the scum is removed, add the washed barley and salt and simmer for 35 minutes.

4 Add the remaining ingredients and simmer for 2 hours.

5 Skim the surface of the soup again and allow the broth to stand for at least 24 hours. Reheat, adjust the seasoning and serve.

VARIATION

This soup is just as delicious made with beef or lamb. Substitute 8 oz lean beef or lean lamb tenderloin for the chicken. Trim any fat from the meat and cut into thin strips before using.

COOK'S TIP

Use either whole-grain barley or pearl barley. Only the outer husk is removed from whole-grain barley and when cooked it has a nutty flavor and a chewy texture.

Open Chicken Sandwiches

These tasty sandwiches are good as a snack on their own or they can be served as part of a picnic spread.

Serves 6

INGREDIENTS

6 thick slices of bread or a large
    French stick cut lengthways, then
    cut into 6 pieces and buttered
3 hard-cooked eggs, the yolk sieved
    & the white chopped

2 tbsp butter, softened
2 tbsp English mustard
1 tsp anchovy extract
2 cups grated Cheddar cheese
3 cooked, skinless chicken breasts,
    chopped finely

12 slices each of tomato and
    cucumber
pepper

1 Remove the crusts from the bread (optional).

2 Reserve the yolk and the white separately from 1 egg.

3 In a large bowl, mix the remaining egg with the softened butter, English mustard, and anchovy extract, and season well with pepper.

4 Mix in the grated Cheddar cheese and chicken and spread the mixture on the bread.

5 Make alternate rows of the egg yolk and the egg white on top of the chicken mixture. Arrange the tomato and cucumber slices on top of the egg and serve.

COOK'S TIP

To soften butter, let it stand at room temperature for 30 minutes or, if you are short of time, cream it in a bowl with a fork. Alternatively, there are now varieties of soft butter available from supermarkets.

COOK'S TIP

If you prefer a less spicy flavor, use a milder mustard. Add mayonnaise if wished and garnish with watercress.

VARIATION

Add 1¾ oz finely chopped broiled bacon to the chicken and cheese mixture for a crunchier texture.

Chicken Pan Bagna

Perfect for a picnic or packed lunch, this Mediterranean-style sandwich can be prepared in advance.

Serves 6

INGREDIENTS

1 large French stick
1 garlic clove
1/2 cup olive oil
3/4 oz canned anchovy fillets

2 oz cold roast chicken
2 large tomatoes, sliced
8 large, pitted black olives, chopped
pepper

1 Using a sharp bread knife, cut the French stick in half lengthways and open out.

2 Cut the garlic clove in half and rub over the bread.

3 Sprinkle the cut surface of the bread with the olive oil.

4 Drain the anchovies and set aside.

5 Thinly slice the chicken and arrange on top of the bread. Arrange the tomatoes and drained anchovies on top of the chicken.

6 Scatter with the chopped black olives and plenty of black pepper. Sandwich the loaf back together and wrap tightly in foil until required. Cut into slices to serve.

VARIATION

You could use Italian ciabatta or olive-studded focaccia bread instead of the French stick, if you prefer. The last few years have seen a veritable interest in different breads and supermarkets now stock a wide range from home and abroad.

COOK'S TIP

Arrange a few fresh basil leaves in between the tomato slices to add a warm, spicy flavor. Use a good quality olive oil in this recipe for extra flavor.

Chicken Rarebit

A tasty dish that can be served alone as a snack or to accompany a light, clear soup.

Serves 4

INGREDIENTS

2 cups grated crumbly cheese
1¹/₃ cups shredded,
  cooked chicken
1 tbsp butter
1 tbsp Worcestershire sauce
1 tsp dry English mustard

2 tsp all-purpose flour
4 tbsp mild beer
4 slices of bread
salt and pepper

1 tbsp chopped fresh parsley, to
  garnish
cherry tomatoes, to serve

1 Place the grated crumbly cheese, chicken, butter, Worcestershire sauce, mustard, all-purpose flour, and beer in a small saucepan. Mix all the ingredients together then season with salt and pepper to taste.

2 Gently bring the mixture to a boil and remove from the heat immediately.

3 Using a wooden spoon, beat until the mixture becomes creamy in texture. Allow it to cool.

4 Once the chicken mixture has cooled, toast the bread on both sides and spread with the chicken mixture.

5 Place under a hot broiler until bubbling and golden brown.

6 Sprinkle with a little chopped parsley and serve with cherry tomatoes.

COOK'S TIP

This is a variation of Welsh rarebit, which does not traditionally contain chicken. Welsh rarebit topped with a poached egg is called buck rarebit.

Chicken & Cheese Jackets

Use the breasts from a roasted chicken for this delicious, healthy snack. Served with a mixed salad,
it is an ideal light meal for a summer's day.

Serves 4

INGREDIENTS

4 large baking potatoes
9 oz cooked, boneless
   chicken breasts
4 scallions

1 cup low-fat soft cheese or Quark
pepper

coleslaw, green salad, or a mixed
salad, to serve

1 Scrub the potatoes and prick them all over with a fork. Bake in a preheated oven, 400°F, for about 50 minutes until tender, or cook in a microwave on high power for 12–15 minutes.

2 Using a sharp knife, dice the chicken, trim and thickly slice the scallions, and mix with the low-fat soft cheese or Quark.

3 Cut a cross through the top of each potato and pull slightly apart. Spoon the chicken filling into the potatoes and sprinkle with freshly ground black pepper. Serve immediately with coleslaw, green salad, or a mixed salad.

VARIATION

For another delicious filling, fry 9 oz button mushrooms in a little butter. Mix with the chicken then add ⅔ cup unsweetened yogurt, 1 tbsp tomato paste, and 2 tsp mild curry powder. Blend well and use to fill the jackets.

COOK'S TIP

Look for Quark in the chilled section. It is a low-fat, white, fresh, curd cheese made from cow's milk with a delicate, slightly sour flavor.

Tuscan Chicken Livers on Toast

Crostini are small pieces of toast with a savoury topping.
In Italy this is a popular antipasto dish.

Serves 4

INGREDIENTS

2 tbsp olive oil
1 garlic clove, finely chopped
8 oz fresh or frozen chicken livers

4 fresh sage leaves, finely chopped,
   or 1 tsp dried, crumbled sage
2 tbsp white wine
2 tbsp lemon juice

salt and pepper
4 slices ciabatta or other Italian
   bread
wedges of lemon, to garnish

1 Heat the olive oil in a skillet and cook the garlic for 1 minute.

2 Rinse and roughly chop the chicken livers, using a sharp knife.

3 Add the chicken liver to the skillet together with the white wine and lemon juice. Cook for 3–4 minutes or until the juices from the chicken liver run clear.

4 Stir in the sage and season to taste with salt and pepper.

5 Under a preheated broiler, toast the bread for 2 minutes on both sides or until golden-brown.

6 Spoon the hot chicken livers on top of the toasted bread and serve garnished with a wedge of lemon.

COOK'S TIP

Overcooked liver is dry and tasteless. Cook the chopped liver for only 3–4 minutes – it should be soft and tender.

VARIATION

Another way to make crostini is to slice a crusty loaf or a French loaf into small rounds or squares. Heat the olive oil in a skillet and fry the slices of bread until golden brown and crisp on both sides. Remove the crostini from the pan with a draining spoon and leave to drain on paper towels. Top with the chicken livers.

Spicy Chicken Livers with Pak Choi

This is a richly flavored dish with a dark, slightly tangy
sauce which is popular in China.

Serves 4

INGREDIENTS

12 oz chicken livers
2 tbsp sunflower oil
1 red chili, seeded and finely chopped
1 tsp fresh grated gingerroot

2 cloves garlic, minced
2 tbsp tomato catsup
3 tbsp sherry
3 tbsp soy sauce

1 tsp cornstarch
1 lb pak choi
egg noodles, to serve

1 Using a sharp knife, trim the fat from the chicken livers and slice into small pieces.

2 Heat the oil in a large wok. Add the chicken liver pieces and stir-fry over a high heat for 2–3 minutes.

3 Add the chili, ginger, and garlic and stir-fry for about 1 minute.

4 Mix together the tomato ketchup, sherry, soy sauce, and cornstarch in a small bowl and set aside.

5 Add the pak choi to the wok and stir-fry until it just wilts.

6 Add the reserved tomato catsup mixture to the wok and cook, stirring to mix, until the juices start to bubble.

7 Transfer to serving bowls and serve hot with noodles.

COOK'S TIP

Fresh gingerroot will keep for several weeks in a dry, cool place.

COOK'S TIP

Chicken livers are available fresh or frozen from most supermarkets.

Chicken & Herb Fritters

These fritters are delicious served with a green salad,
a fresh vegetable salsa or a chili sauce dip.

Makes 8

INGREDIENTS

1 lb 2 oz mashed potato,
  with butter added
1 1/3 cups chopped, cooked chicken
2/3 cups cooked ham, chopped finely
1 tbsp mixed herbs

2 eggs, lightly beaten
milk
2 cups fresh brown bread crumbs
oil for shallow frying
salt and pepper

sprig of fresh parsley, to garnish
mixed salad, to serve

1 In a large bowl, blend the potatoes, chicken, ham, herbs, and 1 egg, and season well.

2 Shape the mixture into small balls or flat pancakes.

3 Add a little milk to the second egg.

4 Place the bread crumbs on a plate. Dip the balls in the egg and milk mixture and roll in the bread crumbs, to coat them completely.

5 Heat the cooking oil in a large skillet and cook the fritters until they are golden brown. Garnish with fresh parsley and serve with a mixed salad.

COOK'S TIP

A mixture of chopped
fresh tarragon and parsley makes a
fresh and flavorful addition
to these fritters.

COOK'S TIP

To make a tomato sauce to serve with
the fritters, heat 3/4 cup sieved
tomatoes and 4 tbsp dry white wine.
Season, remove from the heat, and
add 4 tbsp unsweetened yogurt.
Return to the heat and add chili
powder to taste.

Oaty Chicken Pieces

*A very low-fat chicken recipe with a refreshingly light, mustard-spiced sauce,
which is ideal for a healthy lunchbox or a light meal with salad.*

Serves 4

INGREDIENTS

$1/3$ cup rolled oats
1 tbsp chopped fresh rosemary
4 skinless chicken quarters
1 egg white
$1/2$ cup natural low-fat fromage
   blanc

2 tsp wholegrain mustard
salt and pepper
grated carrot salad, to serve

1 Mix together the rolled oats, fresh rosemary, and salt and pepper.

2 Brush each piece of chicken evenly with egg white, then coat in the oat mixture. Place on a baking sheet and bake in a preheated oven, 400°F, for about 40 minutes or until the juices run clear when the chicken is pierced.

3 In a bowl, mix together the fromage blanc and wholegrain mustard, season with salt and pepper to taste and serve with the chicken, hot or cold, with a grated carrot salad.

VARIATION

To make oaty chicken nuggets, chop up 4 skinless, boneless chicken breasts into small pieces. Reduce the cooking time by about 10 minutes and test for doneness. These nuggets would be ideal at a picnic, buffet, or children's party.

VARIATION

Add 1 tablespoon sesame or sunflower seeds to the oat mixture for an even-crunchier texture. Experiment with different herbs instead of the rosemary.

Chicken Pepperonata

All the sunshine colors and flavors of the Mediterranean are combined in this easy dish.

Serves 4

INGREDIENTS

8 skinless chicken thighs
2 tbsp whole wheat flour
2 tbsp olive oil
1 small onion, sliced thinly
1 garlic clove, minced

1 each large red, yellow, and green
  bell peppers, sliced thinly
14 oz can chopped tomatoes
1 tbsp chopped oregano
salt and pepper

fresh oregano, to garnish
crusty whole-wheat bread, to serve

1 Remove the skin from the chicken thighs and toss in the flour.

2 Heat the oil in a wide pan and fry the chicken quickly until sealed and lightly browned, then remove from the pan. Add the onion to the pan and gently fry until soft. Add the garlic, bell peppers, tomatoes, and oregano, and bring to a boil, stirring.

3 Arrange the chicken over the vegetables, season well with salt and pepper, cover the pan tightly, and simmer for 20–25 minutes or until the chicken is completely cooked and tender.

4 Season to taste, garnish with oregano, and serve with crusty whole-wheat bread.

COOK'S TIP

If you do not have fresh oregano, use sieved tomatoes with herbs already added.

COOK'S TIP

For extra flavor, halve the peppers and broil under a preheated broiler until the skins are charred. Leave to cool and remove the skins and seeds. Slice the bell peppers thinly and use in the recipe.

Cheesy Garlic Drummers

Ideal for informal parties, these tasty chicken drumsticks can be prepared for cooking a day in advance. Instead of baking the chicken drumsticks, you could cook them on the barbecue instead.

Serves 6

INGREDIENTS

1 tbsp butter	3 tbsp fresh bread crumbs
1 garlic clove, minced	12 chicken drumsticks
3 tbsp chopped fresh parsley	salt and pepper
1/2 cup ricotta cheese	lemon slices, to garnish
4 tbsp grated Parmesan cheese	mixed salad leaves, to serve

1 Melt the butter in a pan. Add the garlic and fry gently, stirring, for 1 minute without browning.

2 Remove the pan from the heat and stir in the parsley, the cheeses, bread crumbs, and salt and pepper to taste.

3 Carefully loosen the skin around the drumsticks.

4 Using a teaspoon, push about 1 tablespoon of the stuffing under the skin of each drumstick.

Arrange the drumsticks in a large baking pan.

5 Bake in a preheated oven, 375°F, for about 45 minutes. Serve hot or cold, garnished with lemon slices.

COOK'S TIP

Any strongly flavored cheese can be used instead of the Parmesan. Try a mature hard cheese or use another Italian cheese, such as pecorino.

COOK'S TIP

Freshly grated Parmesan has more bite than ready-packed grated Parmesan from supermarkets. Grate only as much as you need and wrap the rest up in foil – it will keep for several months in the refrigerator.

Coronation Chicken

This classic salad is good as an appetizer or as part of a buffet.
Mango chutney makes a tasty addition.

Serves 6

INGREDIENTS

4 tbsp olive oil
2 lb chicken meat, diced
²/₃ cup rindless, smoked bacon, diced
12 shallots
2 garlic cloves, minced
1 tbsp mild curry powder

1¹/₄ cups mayonnaise
1 tbsp runny honey
1 tbsp chopped fresh parsley
¹/₂ cup seedless black
  grapes, quartered

pepper
cold saffron rice, to serve

1 Heat the oil in a large skillet and add the chicken, bacon, shallots, garlic, and curry powder. Cook slowly for about 15 minutes.

2 Spoon the mixture into a clean mixing bowl.

3 Allow the mixture to cool completely then season with pepper to taste.

4 Blend the mayonnaise with a little honey, then add the chopped fresh parsley. Toss the chicken in the mixture.

5 Place the mixture in a deep serving dish, garnish with the grapes, and serve with cold saffron rice.

COOK'S TIP

You can use this recipe to fill a jacket potato or as a sandwich filling, but cut the chicken into smaller pieces.

VARIATION

Add 2 tbsp chopped fresh apricots and 2 tbsp slivered almonds to the sauce in step 4. For a healthier version of this dish, replace the mayonnaise with the same quantity of unsweetened yogurt and omit the honey otherwise the sauce will be too runny.

Solomongundy

This recipe is ideally suited as a cold platter for a buffet party or a spectacular starter for a special meal.

Serves 4

INGREDIENTS

1 large lettuce
4 chicken breasts,
   cooked and sliced thinly
8 rollmop herrings and
   their marinade
6 hard-cooked eggs, quartered
$^2/_3$ cup cooked ham, sliced
$2^2/_3$ cups roast beef, sliced

$^2/_3$ cup roast lamb, sliced
1 cup snow peas, cooked
$^3/_4$ cup seedless black grapes,
20 stuffed olives, sliced
12 shallots, boiled
$^1/_2$ cup slivered almonds
$^1/_3$ cup golden raisins
2 oranges

sprig of mint
salt and pepper
fresh crusty bread, to serve

1 Spread out the lettuce leaves on a large oval platter.

2 Arrange the chicken in three sections on the platter.

3 Place the roll mops, eggs, and meats in lines or sections over the remainder of the platter.

4 Use the snow peas, grapes, olives, shallots, almonds, and golden raisins to fill in the spaces between the sections.

5 Grate the peel from the oranges and sprinkle over the whole platter. Peel and slice the oranges and add the orange slices and mint sprig to the platter. Season well with salt and pepper. Sprinkle with the herring marinade and serve.

VARIATION

Should you wish, serve with cold, cooked vegetables, such as sliced beans, baby corn-on-the-cob, and cooked beet.

Potted Smoked Chicken

This recipe can be made a few days ahead and kept chilled until needed. A food processor makes light work of blending the ingredients, but you can pound by hand for a coarser mixture.

Serves 4-6

INGREDIENTS

2¹/₂ cups chopped smoked chicken
pinch each of grated nutmeg and
  mace
¹/₂ cup butter, softened

2 tbsp port
2 tbsp heavy cream
salt and pepper
sprig of fresh parsley, to garnish

brown bread slices and fresh butter,
  to serve

1 Place the smoked chicken in a large bowl with the remaining ingredients, and season with salt and pepper to taste.

2 Pound until the mixture is very smooth or blend in a food processor.

3 Transfer the mixture to individual earthenware pots or one large pot.

4 Cover each pot with buttered baking parchment and weigh down with cans or weights. Chill in the refrigerator for 4 hours.

5 Remove the parchment and cover with clarified butter (see Cook's Tip).

6 Garnish with a sprig of parsley and serve with slices of buttered brown bread.

COOK'S TIP

The Potted Smoked Chicken can be kept in the refrigerator for 2–3 days, but no longer as it does not contain any preservatives. It may be stored in the freezer for a maximum of 1 month.

COOK'S TIP

To make clarified butter: place 1 cup butter in a saucepan and heat gently, skimming off the foam as the butter heats – the sediment will sink to the bottom of the pan. When the butter has completely melted, remove the pan from the heat and leave to stand for at least 4 minutes. Strain the butter through a piece of cheesecloth into a bowl. Allow the butter to cool a little before spooning it over the surface of the potted chicken.

Suprême of Chicken with Pear & Blue Cheese Salad

The sweetness of the pears complements perfectly the sharp taste of the blue cheese in this delicious warm salad.

Serves 6

INGREDIENTS

$^1/_4$ cup olive oil
6 shallots, sliced
1 garlic clove, minced
2 tbsp chopped fresh tarragon
1 tbsp English mustard
6 skinless, boneless chicken breasts
1 tbsp flour
$^2/_3$ cup chicken stock

1 apple, diced finely
1 tbsp chopped walnuts
2 tbsp heavy cream
salt and pepper

SALAD:
$3^1/_2$ cups cooked rice
2 large pears, diced

1 cup blue cheese, diced
1 red bell pepper, diced
1 tbsp chopped fresh cilantro
1 tbsp sesame oil

1 Place the olive oil, shallots, garlic, tarragon, and mustard in a deep bowl. Season well and mix the ingredients together thoroughly.

2 Place the chicken in the marinade to coat completely, cover with plastic wrap and chill in the refrigerator for about 4 hours.

3 Drain the chicken, reserving the marinade. Quickly fry the chicken in a large, deep non-stick skillet for 4 minutes on both sides. Transfer the chicken to a warm serving dish.

4 Add the marinade to the pan, bring to a boil, and sprinkle with the flour. Add the chicken stock, apple, and walnuts and

gently simmer for 5 minutes. Return the chicken to the sauce, add the heavy cream, and cook for 2 minutes.

5 Mix the salad ingredients together, place a little on each plate, and top with a chicken breast and a spoonful of the sauce.

Waldorf Summer Chicken Salad

This colorful and healthy dish is a variation of a classic salad. Served with crusty brown rolls, it is an ideal light meal for a summer's day

Serves 4

INGREDIENTS

1 lb 2 oz red apples, diced
3 tbsp fresh lemon juice
$^2/_3$ cup light mayonnaise
1 head of celery
4 shallots, sliced
1 garlic clove, minced

$^3/_4$ cup walnuts, chopped
1 lb 2 oz cooked chicken, cubed
1 Cos lettuce

pepper
sliced apple and walnuts, to garnish

1 Place the apples in a bowl with the lemon juice and 1 tablespoon of mayonnaise. Leave for 40 minutes.

2 Using a sharp knife, slice the celery very thinly.

3 Add the celery, shallots, garlic, and walnuts to the apple and mix together.

4 Stir in the mayonnaise and blend thoroughly.

5 Add the cooked chicken to the bowl and mix well.

6 Line a glass salad bowl or serving dish with the lettuce leaves. Pile the chicken salad into the center, sprinkle with pepper, and garnish with the apple slices and walnuts.

COOK'S TIP

Soaking the apples in lemon juice prevents discoloration.

COOK'S TIP

Instead of the shallots, use scallions for a milder flavor. Trim the scallions and slice finely.

Old English Spicy Chicken Salad

For this simple, refreshing summer salad you can use leftover roast chicken, or ready-roasted chicken to save time. Add the dressing just before serving, or the spinach will lose its crispness.

Serves 4

INGREDIENTS

9 oz young spinach leaves
3 celery stalks, sliced thinly
$^1/_2$ cucumber
2 scallions
3 tbsp chopped fresh parsley
12 oz boneless, roast chicken, sliced
   thinly

DRESSING:
1 inch piece fresh gingerroot, grated
   finely
3 tbsp olive oil
1 tbsp white wine vinegar
1 tbsp honey
$^1/_2$ tsp ground cinnamon
salt and pepper

smoked almonds, to garnish
   (optional)

1 Thoroughly wash the spinach leaves, then pat dry with paper towels.

2 Using a sharp knife, thinly slice the celery, cucumber, and scallions. Toss in a large bowl with the spinach leaves and parsley.

3 Transfer to serving plates and arrange the chicken on top of the salad.

4 In a screw-topped jar, combine all the dressing ingredients and shake well to mix. Season the dressing with salt and pepper to taste, then pour over the salad. Sprinkle with a few smoked almonds, if using.

VARIATION

Substitute corn salad for the spinach, if you prefer.

VARIATION

Fresh young spinach leaves go particularly well with fruit – try adding a few fresh raspberries or nectarine slices to make an even more refreshing salad.

Quick Dishes

One of the marvellous qualities of chicken is that when it is cut into small pieces, it can be cooked very quickly, which is welcome for those of us who are too busy to spend a lot of time preparing meals. In this section, you can select a tasty nutritious dish that won't take hours to make. Pasta makes a perfect partner for chicken as it is also quick to cook – Italian Chicken Spirals look impressive and will fool guests into thinking that you have spent hours slaving away in the kitchen. Chicken breasts are cooked with a delicious basil, hazelnut, and garlic filling and then served on a bed of pasta, olives and sun-dried tomatoes. Smaller cuts of chicken are also ideal for stir-fries that can be quickly cooked to produce tender, moist, and flavorful chicken. Speedy Peanut Pan-Fry is a crunchy stir-fry that is served with noodles. Risottos are also an excellent choice for when you are in a hurry – this chapter contains two risotto recipes although the variations for risotto are endless.

Chicken Strips & Dips

Very simple to make and easy to eat with fingers, this dish can be served warm for a light lunch or cold as part of a buffet.

Serves 2

INGREDIENTS

2 boneless chicken breasts
2 tbsp all-purpose flour
1 tbsp sunflower oil

PEANUT DIP:
3 tbsp smooth or crunchy
　peanut butter
4 tbsp unsweetened yogurt
1 tsp grated orange peel
orange juice (optional)

TOMATO DIP:
5 tbsp creamy fromage blanc
1 medium tomato
2 tsp tomato paste
1 tsp chopped fresh chives

1　Using a sharp knife, slice the chicken into fairly thin strips and toss in the flour to coat.

2　Heat the oil in a non-stick pan and fry the chicken until golden and thoroughly cooked. Remove the chicken strips from the pan and drain well on paper towels.

3　To make the peanut dip, mix together all the ingredients in a bowl (if liked, add a little orange juice to thin the consistency).

4　To make the tomato dip, chop the tomato and mix with the remaining ingredients.

5　Serve the chicken strips with the dips and a selection of vegetable sticks for dipping.

VARIATION

For a lower-fat alternative, poach the strips of chicken in a small amount of boiling chicken stock for 6–8 minutes.

VARIATION

For a refreshing guacamole dip, combine 1 mashed avocado, 2 finely chopped scallions, 1 chopped tomato, 1 crushed garlic clove, and a squeeze of lemon juice. Remember to add the lemon juice immediately after the avocado has been mashed to prevent discoloration.

Quick Chicken Bake

This recipe is a type of cottage pie and is just as versatile. Add vegetables and herbs of your choice, depending on what you have at hand.

Serves 4

INGREDIENTS

1 lb 2 oz ground chicken
1 large onion, chopped finely
2 carrots, diced finely
2 tbsp all-purpose flour
1 tbsp tomato paste

1^1/$_4$ cups chicken stock
pinch of fresh thyme

2 lb potatoes, creamed with butter
  and milk and highly seasoned
^{3}/$_4$ cup grated crumbly cheese
salt and pepper
peas, to serve

1 Dry-fry the ground chicken, onion and carrots in a non-stick saucepan for 5 minutes, stirring frequently.

2 Sprinkle the chicken with the flour and simmer for a further 2 minutes.

3 Gradually blend in the tomato paste and stock then simmer for 15 minutes. Season and add the thyme.

4 Transfer the chicken and vegetable mixture to an ovenproof casserole and allow to cool.

5 Spoon the mashed potato over the chicken mixture and sprinkle with the cheese. Bake in a preheated oven, 400°F, for 20 minutes, or until the cheese is bubbling and golden, then serve with the peas.

VARIATION

Try using a mixture of cheeses on top of this dish. Either use whatever variety of cheese you have to hand in the storecupboard or choose cheeses that melt easily to provide an extra tasty layer of melted cheese on top of the bake.

Tom's Toad in the Hole

This unusual recipe uses chicken and Cumberland sausage,
which is then made into individual bite-sized cakes.

Serves 4–6

INGREDIENTS

1 cup all-purpose flour	1 scant cup milk	9 oz chicken breasts
pinch of salt	$\frac{1}{3}$ cup water	9 oz Cumberland sausage
1 egg, beaten	2 tbsp beef drippings	

1 Mix the flour and salt in a bowl, make a well in the center and add the beaten egg.

2 Add half the milk, and using a wooden spoon, work in the flour slowly.

3 Beat the mixture until smooth, then add the remaining milk and water.

4 Beat again until the mixture is smooth. Let the mixture stand for at least 1 hour.

5 Add the drippings to individual baking pans or to one large baking pan. Cut up the chicken and sausage so that you get a generous piece in each individual pan or several scattered around the large pan.

6 Heat in a preheated oven, 425°F, for 5 minutes until very hot. Remove the pans from the oven and pour in the batter, leaving space for the mixture to expand.

7 Return to the oven to cook for 35 minutes, until risen and golden brown. Do not open the oven door for at least 30 minutes.

8 Serve while hot, with chicken or onion gravy, or alone.

VARIATION

Use skinless, boneless chicken legs instead of chicken breast in the recipe. Cut up as directed. Instead of Cumberland sausage, use your favorite variety of sausage.

Savory Chicken Sausages

Served with a smooth creamy tomato sauce,
this makes an excellent light lunch with freshly baked cheese bread.

Serves 4–6

INGREDIENTS

3 cups fresh bread crumbs
9 oz cooked chicken, ground
1 small leek, chopped finely
pinch each of mixed herbs and
    mustard powder

2 eggs, separated
4 tbsp milk
crisp bread crumbs for coating
2 tbsp beef drippings
salt and pepper

1 In a large clean bowl, combine the bread crumbs, ground chicken, leek, mixed herbs, and mustard powder, and season with salt and pepper. Mix together until thoroughly incorporated.

2 Add 1 whole egg and an egg yolk with a little milk to bind the mixture.

3 Divide the mixture into 6 or 8 and shape into thick or thin sausages.

4 Whisk the remaining egg white until frothy. Coat the sausages first in the egg white and then in the crisp bread crumbs.

5 Heat the drippings and fry the sausages for 6 minutes until golden brown. Serve.

COOK'S TIP

Make your own ground chicken by working lean cuts of chicken in a food processor.

VARIATION

If you want to lower the saturated fat content of this recipe, use a little oil for frying instead of the drippings.

Golden Chicken Risotto

If you prefer, ordinary long grain rice can be used instead of risotto rice, but it won't give you the traditional, deliciously creamy texture that is typical of Italian risottos.

Serves 4

INGREDIENTS

2 tbsp sunflower oil
1 tbsp butter or margarine
1 medium leek, thinly sliced
1 large yellow bell pepper, diced
3 skinless, boneless chicken breasts,
    diced

12 oz risotto rice
few strands saffron
6 $^{1}/_{4}$ cups chicken stock
7 oz can corn-on-the-cob
$^{1}/_{2}$ cup toasted
    unsalted peanuts

$^{1}/_{2}$ cup grated Parmesan cheese
salt and pepper

1 Heat the oil and butter or margarine in a large saucepan. Fry the leek and bell pepper for 1 minute then stir in the chicken and cook, stirring until golden brown.

2 Stir in the rice and cook for 2–3 minutes.

3 Stir in the saffron strands, and salt and pepper to taste.

Add the stock, a little at a time, cover, and cook over a low heat, stirring occasionally, for about 20 minutes, until the rice is tender and most of the liquid is absorbed. Do not let the risotto dry out – add more stock if necessary.

4 Stir in the corn-on-the-cob, peanuts, and Parmesan cheese, then adjust the seasoning to taste. Serve hot.

COOK'S TIP

Risottos can be frozen, before adding the Parmesan cheese, for up to 1 month, but remember to reheat this risotto thoroughly as it contains chicken.

Chicken Risotto alla Milanese

This famous dish is known throughout the world, and it is perhaps the best known of all Italian risottos, although there are many variations.

Serves 4

INGREDIENTS

¹/₂ cup butter

2 lb chicken meat, sliced thinly

1 large onion, chopped

2¹/₂ cups risotto rice

2¹/₂ cups chicken stock

²/₃ cup white wine

1 tsp crumbled saffron

salt and pepper

¹/₂ cup grated
   Parmesan cheese, to serve

1 Heat 4 tbsp of butter in a deep skillet, and fry the chicken, and onion until golden brown.

2 Add the rice, stir well, and cook for 15 minutes.

3 Heat the stock until boiling and gradually add to the rice. Add the white wine, saffron, salt, and pepper to taste and mix well. Simmer gently for 20 minutes, stirring occasionally, and adding more stock if the risotto becomes too dry.

4 Leave to stand for a few minutes and just before serving add a little more stock and simmer for a further 10 minutes. Serve the risotto, sprinkled with the grated Parmesan cheese and the remaining butter.

COOK'S TIP

A risotto should have moist but separate grains. Stock should be added a little at a time and only when the last addition has been completely absorbed.

VARIATION

The possibilities for risotto are endless – try adding the following just at the end of cooking time: cashew nuts and corn, lightly sautéed zucchini and basil, or artichokes and oyster mushrooms.

Golden Glazed Chicken

A glossy glaze with sweet and fruity flavors coats chicken breasts in this tasty recipe.

Serves 6

INGREDIENTS

6 boneless chicken breasts
1 tsp turmeric
1 tbsp whole-grain mustard
1¹/₄ cups orange juice
2 tbsp honey
2 tbsp sunflower oil

1¹/₂ cups long grain rice
1 orange
3 tbsp chopped mint
salt and pepper
mint sprigs, to garnish

1 With a sharp knife, mark the surface of the chicken breasts in a diamond pattern. Mix together the turmeric, mustard, orange juice, and honey and pour over the chicken. Chill until required.

2 Lift the chicken from the marinade and pat dry on paper towels.

3 Heat the oil in a wide pan, add the chicken, and sauté until golden, turning once. Drain off any excess oil. Pour over the marinade, cover, and simmer for 10–15 minutes until the chicken is tender.

4 Boil the rice in lightly salted water until tender and drain well. Finely grate the peel from the orange and stir into the rice with the mint.

5 Using a sharp knife, remove the peel and white pith from the orange and cut the flesh into segments.

6 Serve the chicken with the orange and mint rice, garnished with orange segments and mint sprigs.

VARIATION

To make a slightly sharper sauce, use a small grapefruit instead of the oranges.

Prosciutto-Wrapped Chicken Packets

Stuffed with creamy ricotta, nutmeg, and spinach, then wrapped with wafer thin slices of prosciutto and gently cooked in white wine.

Serves 4

INGREDIENTS

$^1/_2$ cup frozen spinach, defrosted
$^1/_2$ cup ricotta cheese
pinch grated nutmeg
4 skinless, boneless chicken breasts,
   each weighing 6 oz
4 prosciutto slices

2 tbsp butter
1 tbsp olive oil
12 small onions or shallots
$1^1/_2$ cups button
   mushrooms, sliced
1 tbsp all-purpose flour

$^2/_3$ cup dry white or red wine
$1^1/_4$ cups chicken stock
salt and pepper

1 Put the spinach into a strainer and press out the water with a spoon. Mix with the ricotta and nutmeg and season with salt and pepper to taste.

2 Using a sharp knife, slit each chicken breast through the side and enlarge each cut to form a pocket. Fill with the spinach mixture, reshape the chicken breasts, wrap each breast tightly in a slice of ham, and secure with toothpicks. Cover and chill in the refrigerator.

3 Heat the butter and oil in a skillet and brown the chicken breasts for 2 minutes on each side. Transfer the chicken to a large, shallow ovenproof dish and keep warm until required.

4 Fry the onions and mushrooms for 2–3 minutes until lightly browned. Stir in the all-purpose flour then gradually add the wine and stock. Bring to a boil, stirring constantly. Season and spoon the mixture around the chicken.

5 Cook the chicken uncovered in a preheated oven, 400°F, for 20 minutes. Turn the breasts over and cook for a further 10 minutes. Remove the toothpicks and serve with the sauce, together with carrot paste and green beans, if wished.

Italian Chicken Spirals

Steaming allows you to cook without fat, and these little foil packets retain all the natural juices of the chicken while cooking conveniently over the pasta while it boils.

Serves 4

INGREDIENTS

4 skinless, boneless, chicken breasts
1 cup fresh basil leaves
2 tbsp hazelnuts
1 garlic clove, minced
2 cups whole-wheat pasta spirals

2 sun-dried tomatoes
  or fresh tomatoes
1 tbsp lemon juice
1 tbsp olive oil
1 tbsp capers

$^1/_2$ cup black olives
salt and pepper

1 Beat the chicken breasts with a rolling pin to flatten evenly.

2 Place the basil and hazelnuts in a food processor and process until finely chopped. Mix with the garlic, salt, and pepper.

3 Spread the basil mixture over the chicken breasts and roll up from one short end to enclose the filling. Wrap the chicken roll tightly in foil so that they hold their shape, then seal the ends well.

4 Bring a large pan of lightly salted water to a boil and cook the pasta until tender, but still firm to the bite.

5 Place the chicken packets in a steamer basket or colander set over the pan, cover tightly, and steam for 10 minutes. Meanwhile, dice the tomatoes.

6 Drain the pasta and return to the pan with the lemon juice, olive oil, tomatoes, capers, and olives. Heat through.

7 Pierce the chicken with a skewer to make sure that the juices run clear and not pink, then slice the chicken, arrange over the pasta, and serve.

VARIATION

Sun-dried tomatoes have a wonderful, rich flavor, but if you can't find them, use fresh tomatoes.

Garlicky Chicken Cushions

Stuffed with creamy ricotta, spinach, and garlic, then gently cooked in a rich tomato sauce, this is a suitable dish to make ahead of time.

Serves 4

INGREDIENTS

4 part-boned chicken breasts
$^1/_2$ cup frozen spinach, defrosted
$^1/_2$ cup ricotta cheese
2 garlic cloves, crushed
1 tbsp olive oil
1 onion, chopped

1 red bell pepper, sliced
14 oz can chopped tomatoes
6 tbsp wine or chicken stock
10 stuffed olives, sliced

salt and pepper
pasta, to serve

1 Make a slit between the skin and meat on one side of each chicken breast. Lift the skin to form a pocket, being careful to leave the skin attached to the other side.

2 Put the spinach into a strainer and press out the water with a spoon. Mix with the ricotta, half the garlic, and seasoning.

3 Spoon the spinach mixture under the skin of each chicken breast, then secure the edge of the skin with toothpicks.

4 Heat the oil in a skillet, add the onion, and fry for a minute, stirring. Add the remaining garlic and red bell pepper and cook for 2 minutes. Stir in the tomatoes, wine, or stock, olives and seasoning. Set the sauce aside and chill the chicken if preparing in advance.

5 Bring the sauce to a boil, pour into a shallow ovenproof dish and arrange the chicken breasts on top in a single layer.

6 Cook, uncovered in a preheated oven, 400°F, for 35 minutes until the chicken is golden and cooked through. Test by making a slit in one of the chicken breasts with a skewer to make sure the juices run clear and not pink. Spoon a little of the sauce over the chicken breasts then transfer to serving plates. Serve with pasta.

Mediterranean Chicken Parcels

This method of cooking makes the chicken aromatic and succulent. It also reduces the amount of oil needed since the chicken and vegetables cook in their own juices.

Serves 6

INGREDIENTS

1 tbsp olive oil
6 skinless chicken breast fillets
2 cups Mozzarella cheese

3¹/₂ cups zucchini, sliced
6 large tomatoes, sliced
1 small bunch fresh basil or oregano

pepper
rice or pasta, to serve

1 Cut six pieces of foil each about 10 inches square. Brush the foil squares lightly with oil and set aside until required.

2 With a sharp knife, slash each chicken breast at intervals, slice the Mozzarella cheese, and place between the cuts in the chicken.

3 Divide the zucchini and tomatoes between the pieces of foil and sprinkle with black pepper. Tear or roughly chop the basil or oregano and scatter over the vegetables in each packet.

4 Place the chicken on top of each pile of vegetables then wrap in the foil to enclose the chicken and vegetables, tucking in the ends.

5 Place on a cookie sheet and bake in a preheated oven, 400°C, for about 30 minutes.

6 To serve, unwrap each foil packet and serve with rice or pasta.

COOK'S TIP

To aid cooking, place the vegetables and chicken on the shiny side of the foil so that once the packet is wrapped up the dull surface of the foil is facing outward. This ensures that the heat is absorbed into the packet and not reflected away from it.

Steamed Chicken & Spring Vegetable Packets

A healthy recipe with a delicate oriental flavor, ideal for tender young summer vegetables.
You'll need large spinach leaves to wrap around the chicken, but make sure they are young leaves.

Serves 4

INGREDIENTS

4 boneless, skinless
   chicken breasts
1 tsp ground lemongrass
2 scallions, chopped finely

1 cup young carrots
1³/₄ cups young zucchini
2 stalks celery
1 tsp light soy sauce

³/₄ cup spinach leaves
2 tsp sesame oil
salt and pepper

1 With a sharp knife, make a slit through one side of each chicken breast, to open out a large pocket. Sprinkle the inside of the pocket with lemongrass, salt, and pepper. Tuck the scallions into the pockets.

2 Trim the carrots, zucchini, and celery and cut into small matchsticks. Plunge them into a pan of boiling water for 1 minute, drain, and toss in the soy sauce.

3 Pack the vegetables into the pockets in each chicken breast and fold over firmly to enclose. Reserve any remaining vegetables. Wash the spinach leaves thoroughly, drain, and pat dry with paper towels. Wrap the chicken breasts firmly in the spinach leaves to enclose completely. If the leaves are too firm to wrap the chicken easily, steam them for a few seconds until they are softened and flexible.

4 Place the wrapped chicken in a steamer and steam over rapidly boiling water for 20–25 minutes, depending on size.

5 Stir-fry any leftover vegetable sticks and spinach for 1–2 minutes in the sesame oil and serve with the chicken.

Chicken with Two Bell Pepper Sauce

This quick and simple dish is colorful and healthy.
It would be perfect for an impromptu lunch or supper dish.

Serves 4

INGREDIENTS

2 tbsp olive oil
2 medium onions, chopped finely
2 garlic cloves, minced
2 red bell peppers, chopped
good pinch cayenne pepper
2 tsp tomato paste

2 yellow bell peppers, chopped
pinch of dried basil
4 skinless, boneless
  chicken breasts
$^2/_3$ cup dry white wine
$^2/_3$ cup chicken stock

bouquet garni
salt and pepper
fresh herbs, to garnish

1 Heat 1 tablespoon of oil in each of two medium-sized saucepans. Place half the chopped onions, 1 of the garlic cloves, the red bell peppers, the cayenne pepper, and the tomato paste in one of the saucepans. Place the remaining onion, garlic, yellow bell peppers, and basil in the other pan.

2 Cover each pan and cook over a very low heat for 1 hour until the bell peppers are soft. If either mixture becomes dry, add a little water. Work each mixture separately in a food processor, then sift separately.

3 Return the separate mixtures to the pans and season. The two sauces can be gently re-heated while the chicken is cooking.

4 Put the chicken breasts into a skillet and add the wine and stock. Add the bouquet garni and bring the liquid to simmer. Cook the chicken for about 20 minutes until tender.

5 To serve, pour a serving of each sauce on to four serving plates, slice the chicken breasts, and arrange on the plates. Garnish with fresh herbs.

COOK'S TIP

Make your own bouquet garni by tying together sprigs of your favorite herbs with string, or wrap up dried herbs in a piece of muslin. A popular combination is thyme, parsley, and bay.

Harlequin Chicken

This colorful, simple dish will tempt the appetites of all the family – it is ideal for toddlers, who enjoy the fun shapes of the multi-colored bell peppers.

Serves 4

INGREDIENTS

10 skinless, boneless chicken thighs
1 medium onion
1 each medium red, green, and yellow bell peppers
1 tbsp sunflower oil

14 oz can chopped tomatoes
2 tbsp chopped fresh parsley
pepper

whole wheat bread and a green salad, to serve

1 Using a sharp knife, cut the chicken thighs into bite-sized pieces.

2 Peel and thinly slice the onion. Halve and seed the bell peppers and cut into small diamond shapes.

3 Heat the oil in a shallow skillet. Add the chicken and onion and fry quickly until golden.

4 Add the bell peppers, cook for 2–3 minutes, stir in the tomatoes and parsley, and season with pepper.

5 Cover tightly and simmer for about 15 minutes, until the chicken and vegetables are tender. Serve hot with whole wheat bread and a green salad.

COOK'S TIP

You can use dried parsley instead of fresh but remember that you only need about one half of dried to fresh.

COOK'S TIP

If you are making this dish for small children, the chicken can be finely chopped or ground first.

Elizabethan Chicken

Chicken is surprisingly delicious when combined
with fruits such as grapes or gooseberries.

Serves 4

INGREDIENTS

1 tbsp butter

1 tbsp sunflower oil

4 skinless, boneless
   chicken breasts

4 shallots, finely chopped

²/₃ cup chicken stock

1 tbsp cider vinegar

1 cup halved seedless grapes

¹/₂ cup heavy cream

1 tsp freshly grated nutmeg

cornstarch, to thicken, (optional)

salt and pepper

1 Heat the butter and sunflower oil in a wide, flameproof casserole or pan and quickly fry the chicken breasts until golden brown, turning once. Remove the chicken breasts and keep warm while you are cooking the shallots.

2 Add the chopped shallots to the pan and fry gently until softened and lightly browned. Return the chicken breasts to the pan.

3 Add the chicken stock and cider vinegar to the pan, bring to a boil, cover, and simmer gently for 10–12 minutes, stirring occasionally.

4 Transfer the chicken to a serving dish. Add the grapes, cream, and nutmeg to the pan. Heat through, seasoning with salt and pepper to taste. Add a little cornstarch to thicken the sauce, if desired. Pour the sauce over the chicken and serve.

VARIATION

If desired, add a little dry white
wine or vermouth to the sauce
in step 3.

Poached Breast of Chicken with Whisky Sauce

After cooking with stock and vegetables, chicken breasts are served with a velvety sauce made from whiskey and crème fraîche.

Serves 6

INGREDIENTS

2 tbsp butter

$^1/_2$ cup shredded leeks

$^1/_3$ cup diced carrot

$^1/_4$ cup diced celery

4 shallots, sliced

$2^1/_2$ cups chicken stock

6 chicken breasts

$^1/_4$ cup whiskey

1 scant cup crème fraîche

2 tbsp freshly grated horseradish

1 tsp honey, warmed

1 tsp chopped fresh parsley

salt and pepper

sprig of fresh parsley, to garnish

1 Melt the butter in a large saucepan and add the leeks, carrot, celery, and shallots. Cook for 3 minutes, add half the chicken stock, and cook for about 8 minutes.

2 Add the remaining chicken stock, bring to a boil, add the chicken breasts, and cook for 10 minutes.

3 Remove the chicken and thinly slice. Place on a large, hot serving dish and keep warm until required.

4 In another saucepan, heat the whiskey until reduced by half. Strain the chicken stock through a fine sifter, add to the pan, and reduce the liquid by half.

5 Add the crème fraîche, the horseradish, and the honey. Heat gently and add the chopped parsley and salt and pepper to taste. Stir until well blended.

6 Pour a little of the whiskey sauce around the chicken and pour the remaining sauce into a sauceboat to serve.

7 Serve with a vegetable patty made from the leftover vegetables, mashed potato, and fresh vegetables. Garnish with the parsley sprig.

Devilled Chicken

Chicken is spiked with cayenne pepper and paprika and finished off with a fruity sauce.

Serves 2-3

INGREDIENTS

$^1/_4$ cup all-purpose flour
1 tbsp cayenne pepper
1 tsp paprika
12 oz skinless, boneless chicken, diced
2 tbsp butter

1 onion, chopped finely
$1^7/_8$ cups milk, warmed
4 tbsp apple paste

$^3/_4$ cup white grapes
$^2/_3$ cup soured cream
sprinkle of paprika

1 Mix the flour, cayenne pepper, and paprika together and use to coat the chicken.

2 Shake off any excess flour. Melt the butter in a saucepan and gently fry the chicken with the onion for 4 minutes.

3 Stir in the flour and spice mixture. Add the milk slowly, stirring until the sauce thickens.

4 Simmer until the sauce is smooth.

5 Add the apple paste and grapes and simmer gently for 20 minutes.

6 Transfer the chicken and devilled sauce to a serving dish and top with soured cream and a sprinkle of paprika.

VARIATION

For a healthier alternative to soured cream, use unsweetened yogurt.

COOK'S TIP

Add more paprika if desired – as it is quite a mild spice, you can add plenty without it being too overpowering.

Chicken Lady Jayne

If you prefer, just use boneless chicken breasts in this recipe.
This dish has a surprising combination of coffee and brandy flavors.

Serves 4

INGREDIENTS

4 chicken breasts or suprêmes, each
   about 4¹/₂ oz
4 tbsp corn oil
8 shallots, sliced
peel and juice of 1 lemon

2 tsp Worcestershire sauce
4 tbsp chicken stock
1 tbsp chopped fresh parsley
3 tbsp coffee liqueur
3 tbsp brandy, warmed

1 Place the chicken breasts or suprêmes on a chopping board, cover with plastic wrap and pound them until flattened with a meat mallet or rolling pin.

2 Heat the oil in a large skillet and fry the chicken for 3 minutes on each side. Add the shallots and cook for a further 3 minutes.

3 Sprinkle with lemon juice and lemon peel and add the Worcestershire sauce and chicken stock. Cook for 2 minutes, then sprinkle with the chopped fresh parsley.

4 Add the coffee liqueur and the brandy and flame the chicken by lighting the spirit with a taper or long match. Cook until the flame is extinguished and serve.

COOK'S TIP

A suprême is a chicken fillet that sometimes has part of the wing bone remaining. Chicken breasts can be used instead.

COOK'S TIP

Flattening the suprêmes means that they take less time to cook.

Chicken, Corn, & Snow Pea Stir-Fry

This quick and healthy dish is stir-fried, which means you need use only the minimum of fat. If you don't have a wok, use a wide skillet instead.

Serves 4

INGREDIENTS

4 skinless, boneless
  chicken breasts
1¹/₃ cups baby corn-on-the-cob
9 oz snow peas

2 tbsp sunflower oil
1 tbsp sherry vinegar
1 tbsp honey
1 tbsp light soy sauce

1 tbsp sunflower seeds
pepper
rice or egg noodles, to serve

1 Using a sharp knife, slice the chicken breasts into long, thin strips. Cut the baby corn-on-the-cob in half lengthways and top and tail the snow peas. Set the vegetables aside until required.

2 Heat the sunflower oil in a wok or a wide skillet and fry the chicken over a fairly high heat, stirring constantly, for 1 minute.

3 Add the corn and snow peas and stir over a medium heat for 5–8 minutes, until evenly cooked.

4 Mix together the sherry vinegar, honey, and soy sauce and stir into the pan with the sunflower seeds. Season with pepper to taste. Cook, stirring constantly, for 1 minute. Serve the sauté hot with rice or Chinese egg noodles.

COOK'S TIP

Rice vinegar or balsamic vinegar makes a good substitute for the sherry vinegar.

Speedy Peanut Pan-Fry

A complete main course cooked within ten minutes. Thread egg noodles are the ideal accompaniment because they can be cooked quickly and easily while the stir-fry sizzles.

Serves 4

INGREDIENTS

2 cups zucchini
1¹/₃ cups baby corn-on-the-cob
3³/₄ cups button mushrooms
3 cups thread egg noodles
2 tbsp corn oil

1 tbsp sesame oil
8 boneless chicken thighs
  or 4 breasts, sliced thinly
1¹/₂ cups beansprouts ·
4 tbsp smooth peanut butter

2 tbsp soy sauce
2 tbsp lime or lemon juice
¹/₂ cup roasted peanuts
pepper
cilantro, to garnish

1 Using a sharp knife, trim and thinly slice the zucchini, corn-on-the-cob, and button mushrooms.

2 Bring a large pan of lightly salted boiling water to a boil and cook the noodles for 3–4 minutes. Meanwhile, heat the corn oil and sesame oil in a large skillet or wok and fry the chicken over a high heat for 1 minute.

3 Add the sliced zucchini, corn-on-the-cob, and button mushrooms and stir-fry for 5 minutes.

4 Add the beansprouts, peanut butter, soy sauce, lime or lemon juice, and pepper, then cook for a further 2 minutes.

5 Drain the noodles, transfer to a serving dish, and scatter with the peanuts. Serve with the stir-fried chicken and vegetables, garnished with a sprig of cilantro.

COOK'S TIP

Try serving this stir-fry with rice sticks. These are broad, pale, translucent ribbon noodles made from ground rice.

Chicken, Bell Pepper, & Orange Stir-Fry

Chicken thighs are inexpensive, meaty portions of the chicken which are readily available.
The meat is not as tender as the breast but it is perfect for stir-frying.

Serves 4

INGREDIENTS

3 tbsp sunflower oil
12 oz boneless chicken thighs,
  skinned and cut into thin strips
1 onion, sliced
1 clove garlic, minced

1 red bell pepper, seeded and sliced
1¼ cups snow peas
4 tbsp light soy sauce
4 tbsp sherry
1 tbsp tomato paste
finely grated peel and juice of 1 orange

1 tsp cornstarch
2 oranges
1 cup beansprouts
cooked rice or noodles, to serve

1 Heat the sunflower oil in a large preheated wok.

2 Add the strips of chicken to the wok and stir-fry for 2–3 minutes or until sealed on all sides.

3 Add the sliced onion, garlic, bell pepper, and snow peas to the wok. Stir-fry the mixture for a further 5 minutes, or until the vegetables are just becoming tender and the chicken is completely cooked through.

4 Mix together the soy sauce, sherry, tomato paste, orange peel and juice, and the cornstarch in a measuring pitcher.

5 Add the mixture to the wok and cook, stirring, until the juices start to thicken.

6 Using a sharp knife, peel and segment the oranges.

7 Add the orange segments and beansprouts to the mixture in the wok and heat through for a further 2 minutes.

8 Transfer the stir-fry to serving plates and serve at once with cooked rice or noodles.

COOK'S TIP

Beansprouts are sprouting mung beans and are a regular ingredient in Chinese cooking. They require very little cooking and may even be eaten raw, if wished.

Stir-Fried Chicken with Chili & Crispy Basil

Chicken drumsticks are cooked in a delicious sauce and served with deep-fried basil for color and flavor.

Serves 4

INGREDIENTS

8 chicken drumsticks
2 tbsp soy sauce
1 tbsp sunflower oil
1 red chili

$3\frac{1}{2}$ oz carrots, cut into thin stalks
6 celery stalks, cut into sticks
3 tbsp sweet chili sauce

oil, for frying
about 50 fresh basil leaves

1 Remove the skin from the chicken drumsticks if desired. Make 3 slashes in each drumstick. Brush the drumsticks with the soy sauce.

2 Heat the oil in a preheated wok and fry the drumsticks for 20 minutes, turning frequently, until they are cooked through.

3 Seed and finely chop the chili. Add the chili, carrots, and celery to the wok and cook for a further 5 minutes. Stir in the chili sauce, cover, and allow to bubble gently whilst preparing the basil leaves.

4 Heat a little oil in a heavy based pan. Carefully add the basil leaves – stand well away from the pan and protect your hand with a dish cloth as they may spit a little. Cook for about 30 seconds or until they begin to curl up but not brown. Transfer to kitchen paper to drain.

5 Arrange the cooked chicken, vegetables and pan juices on to a warm serving plate and garnish with the deep-fried crispy basil leaves.

COOK'S TIP

Basil has a very strong flavor which is perfect with chicken and Chinese flavorings. You could use baby spinach instead of the basil, if you prefer.

Coconut Chicken Curry

Okra or ladies fingers are slightly bitter in flavor. The pineapple and coconut in this recipe offsets them in both color and flavor.

Serves 4

INGREDIENTS

2 tbsp sunflower oil or 1 oz ghee
1 lb boneless, skinless chicken thighs
  or breasts
1 cup okra
1 large onion, sliced
2 cloves garlic, minced

3 tbsp mild curry paste
$2^1/4$ cups chicken stock
1 tbsp fresh lemon juice
$1/2$ cup creamed coconut
$1^1/4$ cups fresh or canned pineapple,
  cubed
$2/3$ cup thick, unsweetened yogurt
2 tbsp chopped fresh cilantro

freshly boiled rice, to serve

TO GARNISH:
lemon wedges
fresh cilantro sprigs

1 Heat the sunflower oil or ghee in a large preheated wok.

2 Using a sharp knife, cut the chicken into bite-sized pieces. Add the chicken to the wok and cook, stirring frequently, until evenly browned.

3 Using a sharp knife, trim the okra.

4 Add the onion, garlic, and okra to the wok and cook

for a further 2–3 minutes, stirring constantly.

5 Mix the curry paste with the chicken stock and lemon juice and pour over the mixture in the wok. Bring to a boil, cover, and leave to simmer for 30 minutes.

6 Coarsely grate the creamed coconut, stir it into the curry, and cook for about 5 minutes – the creamed coconut will help to thicken the juices.

7 Add the pineapple, yogurt, and cilantro and heat through for 2 minutes, stirring.

8 Garnish and serve hot with boiled rice.

COOK'S TIP

Score around the top of the okra with a knife before cooking to release the sticky glue-like substance which is bitter in taste.

Stir-Fried Garlic Chicken with Cilantro & Lime

Garlic and cilantro butter flavors and moistens chicken breasts which are served with a caramelized sauce, sharpened with lime juice.

Serves 4

INGREDIENTS

4 large skinless, boneless chicken
   breasts
3 tbsp garlic butter, softened
3 tbsp chopped fresh cilantro

1 tbsp sunflower oil
finely grated peel and juice of 2 limes
4 tbsp palm sugar or demerara sugar
boiled rice, to serve

1 Place each chicken breast between 2 sheets of plastic wrap and pound with a rolling pin until flattened to ½ inch thick.

2 Mix together the garlic butter and cilantro and spread over each flattened chicken breast. Roll up and secure with a toothpick.

3 Heat the oil in a wok. Add the chicken rolls and cook, turning, for 15–20 minutes or until cooked through.

4 Remove the chicken from the wok and transfer to a board. Cut each chicken roll into slices.

5 Add the lime peel, juice, and sugar to the wok and heat gently, stirring, until the sugar has dissolved. Raise the heat and allow to bubble for 2 minutes.

6 Arrange the chicken on warmed serving plates and spoon the pan juices over to serve.

7 Garnish with extra cilantro if desired.

COOK'S TIP

Be sure to check that the chicken is cooked through before slicing and serving. Cook over a gentle heat so as not to overcook the outside, while the inside remains raw.

Chicken, Spring Green, & Yellow Bean Stir-Fry

Yellow bean sauce is made from yellow soy beans and is available in most supermarkets.
Try to buy a chunky sauce rather than a smooth sauce for texture.

Serves 4

INGREDIENTS

2 tbsp sunflower oil
1 lb skinless, boneless chicken breasts
2 cloves garlic, minced

1 green bell pepper

$1^{1}/_{2}$ cups snow peas
6 scallions, sliced, plus extra to garnish
8 oz spring greens or cabbage, shredded

$5^{3}/_{4}$ oz jar yellow bean sauce
3 tbsp roasted cashew nuts

1 Heat the sunflower oil in a large preheated wok.

2 Using a sharp knife, slice the chicken into thin strips.

3 Add the chicken to the wok together with the garlic. Stir-fry for about 5 minutes or until the chicken is sealed on all sides and beginning to turn golden.

4 Using a sharp knife, seed the green bell pepper and cut into thin strips.

5 Add the snow peas, scallions, green bell pepper strips, and spring greens or cabbage to the wok. Stir-fry for a further 5 minutes or until the vegetables are just tender.

6 Stir in the yellow bean sauce and heat through for about 2 minutes or until the mixture starts to bubble.

7 Scatter with the roasted cashew nuts.

8 Transfer the chicken, spring green, and yellow bean stir-fry to warm serving plates and garnish with extra scallions, if desired. Serve the stir-fry immediately.

COOK'S TIP

Do not add salted cashew nuts to this dish, otherwise when combined with the slightly salty sauce, the dish will be very salty indeed.

Chicken Stir-Fry with Cumin Seeds & Trio of Bell Peppers

Cumin seeds are more frequently associated with Indian cooking, but they are used in this Chinese recipe for their earthy flavor. You could use ¹/₂ tsp of ground cumin instead.

Serves 4

INGREDIENTS

1 lb boneless, skinless chicken breasts
2 tbsp sunflower oil
1 clove garlic, minced
1 tbsp cumin seeds
1 tbsp grated fresh gingerroot

1 red chili, seeded and sliced
1 red bell pepper, seeded and sliced
1 green bell pepper, seeded and sliced
1 yellow bell pepper, seeded and sliced
1 cup beansprouts
12 oz pak choi or other green leaves

2 tbsp sweet chili sauce
3 tbsp light soy sauce
deep-fried crispy ginger, to garnish
  (see Cook's Tip)

1 Using a sharp knife, slice the chicken breasts into thin strips.

2 Heat the oil in a large preheated wok.

3 Add the chicken to the wok and stir-fry for 5 minutes.

4 Add the garlic, cumin seeds, ginger, and chili to the wok, stirring to mix.

5 Add all of the bell peppers to the wok and stir-fry for a further 5 minutes.

6 Toss in the beansprouts and pak choi together with the sweet chili sauce and soy sauce and continue to cook until the pak choi leaves start to wilt.

7 Transfer to warm serving bowls and garnish with deep-fried ginger (see Cook's Tip).

COOK'S TIP

To make the deep-fried ginger garnish, peel, and thinly slice a large piece of gingerroot, using a sharp knife. Carefully lower the slices of ginger into a wok or small pan of hot oil and cook for about 30 seconds. Remove the deep-fried ginger with a draining spoon, transfer to sheets of paper towels and leave to drain thoroughly.

Thai Red Chicken with Cherry Tomatoes

This is a really colorful dish, the red of the tomatoes perfectly complementing the orange sweet potato.

Serves 4

INGREDIENTS

1 tbsp sunflower oil
1 lb boneless, skinless chicken
2 cloves garlic, minced
2 tbsp Thai red curry paste
2 tbsp fresh grated galangal or
   gingerroot

1 tbsp tamarind paste
4 lime leaves
8 oz sweet potato
2$^1/_2$ cups coconut milk
8 oz cherry tomatoes, halved

3 tbsp chopped fresh cilantro
cooked jasmine or Thai fragrant rice,
   to serve

1 Heat the sunflower oil in a large preheated wok.

2 Thinly slice the chicken. Add the chicken to the wok and stir-fry for 5 minutes.

3 Add the garlic, curry paste, galangal or root ginger, tamarind, and lime leaves to the wok and stir-fry for 1 minute.

4 Using a sharp knife, peel and dice the sweet potato.

5 Add the coconut milk and sweet potato to the mixture in the wok and bring to a boil. Allow to bubble over a medium heat for 20 minutes, or until the juices start to thicken and reduce.

6 Add the cherry tomatoes and cilantro to the curry and cook for a further 5 minutes, stirring occasionally. Transfer to serving plates and serve hot with cooked jasmine or Thai fragrant rice.

COOK'S TIP

Galangal is a spice very similar to ginger and is used to replace the latter in Thai cuisine. It can be bought fresh from Oriental food stores but is also available dried and as a powder. The fresh root, which is not as pungent as ginger, needs to be peeled before slicing to use.

Peppered Chicken Stir-Fried with Sugar Snap Peas

Crushed mixed peppercorns coat tender, thin strips of chicken which are cooked with green and red bell peppers for a really colorful dish.

Serves 4

INGREDIENTS

2 tbsp tomato catsup

2 tbsp soy sauce

1 lb boneless, skinless chicken breasts

2 tbsp minced mixed peppercorns

2 tbsp sunflower oil

1 red bell pepper

1 green bell pepper

2¹/₂ cups sugar snap peas

2 tbsp oyster sauce

1 Mix the tomato catsup with the soy sauce in a bowl.

2 Using a sharp knife, slice the chicken into thin strips. Toss the chicken in the tomato catsup and soy sauce mixture.

3 Sprinkle the crushed peppercorns on to a plate. Dip the coated chicken in the peppercorns until evenly coated.

4 Heat the sunflower oil in a preheated wok.

5 Add the chicken to the wok and stir-fry for 5 minutes.

6 Seed and slice the bell peppers.

7 Add the bell peppers to the wok together with the sugar snap peas and stir-fry for a further 5 minutes.

8 Add the oyster sauce and allow to bubble for 2 minutes. Transfer to serving bowls and serve immediately.

VARIATION

Use snow peas instead of sugar snap peas, if you prefer.

Stir-Fried Chicken with Cashew Nuts & Yellow Bean Sauce

Chicken and cashew nuts are a great classic combination, and this recipe is no exception. Flavored with yellow bean sauce, it is a quick and delicious dish.

Serves 4

INGREDIENTS

1 lb boneless chicken breasts
2 tbsp vegetable oil
1 red onion, sliced

1 1/2 cups flat mushrooms, sliced
1/3 cup cashew nuts
2 3/4 oz jar yellow bean sauce

fresh cilantro, to garnish
egg fried rice or plain boiled rice,
   to serve

1 Using a sharp knife, remove the excess skin from the chicken breasts if desired. Cut the chicken into small, bite-sized chunks.

2 Heat the vegetable oil in a preheated wok.

3 Add the chicken to the wok and stir-fry for 5 minutes.

4 Add the red onion and mushrooms to the wok and continue to stir-fry for a further 5 minutes.

5 Place the cashew nuts on a cookie sheet and toast under a preheated medium broiler until just browning – this brings out their flavor.

6 Toss the toasted cashew nuts into the wok together with the yellow bean sauce. Allow the sauce to bubble for 2–3 minutes.

7 Transfer to warm serving bowls and garnish with fresh cilantro. Serve hot with egg fried rice or plain boiled rice.

COOK'S TIP

Chicken thighs could be used instead of the chicken breasts for a more economical dish.

Stir-Fried Chicken with Cumin Seeds & Eggplant

This is a delicious curried chicken and eggplant dish, flavored with tomatoes and seasoned with fresh mint.

Serves 4

INGREDIENTS

5 tbsp sunflower oil
2 cloves garlic, minced
1 tbsp cumin seeds
1 tbsp mild curry powder
1 tbsp paprika

1 lb boneless, skinless chicken breasts
1 large eggplant, cubed
4 tomatoes, cut into quarters
$1/3$ cup chicken stock
1 tbsp fresh lemon juice

$1/2$ tsp salt
$2/3$ cup unsweetened yogurt
1 tbsp chopped fresh mint

1 Heat 2 tablespoons of the sunflower oil in a large preheated wok.

2 Add the garlic, cumin seeds, curry powder, and paprika to the wok and stir-fry for 1 minute.

3 Using a sharp knife, thinly slice the chicken breasts.

4 Add the rest of the oil to the wok and stir-fry the chicken for 5 minutes.

5 Add the eggplant cubes, tomatoes, and chicken stock and bring to a boil. Reduce the heat and leave to simmer for about 20 minutes.

6 Stir in the lemon juice, salt, and yogurt and cook over a gentle heat for a further 5 minutes, stirring occasionally.

7 Scatter with chopped fresh mint and transfer to serving bowls. Serve immediately.

COOK'S TIP

Once the yogurt has been added, do not boil the sauce as it will curdle.

Stir-Fried Ginger Chicken

*The oranges add color and piquancy to this refreshing dish,
which complements the chicken well.*

Serves 4

INGREDIENTS

2 tbsp sunflower oil
1 onion, sliced
6 oz carrots, cut into thin sticks
1 clove garlic, minced

12 oz boneless skinless chicken
  breasts
2 tbsp fresh gingerroot, peeled and
  grated
1 tsp ground ginger
4 tbsp sweet sherry

1 tbsp tomato paste
1 tbsp demerara sugar
1/3 cup orange juice
1 tsp cornstarch
1 orange, peeled and segmented
fresh snipped chives, to garnish

1 Heat the oil in a large preheated wok. Add the onion, carrots, and garlic, and stir-fry over a high heat for 3 minutes or until the vegetables begin to soften.

2 Using a sharp knife, slice the chicken into thin strips. Add the chicken to the wok together with the fresh gingerroot and ground ginger. Stir-fry for a further 10 minutes, or until the chicken is well cooked through and golden in color.

3 Mix together the sherry, tomato paste, sugar, orange juice, and cornstarch in a bowl. Stir the mixture into the wok and heat through until the mixture bubbles and the juices start to thicken.

4 Add the orange segments and carefully toss to mix.

5 Transfer the stir-fried chicken to warm serving bowls and garnish with freshly snipped chives. Serve immediately.

COOK'S TIP

Make sure that you do not continue cooking the dish once the orange segments have been added in step 4, otherwise they will break up.

Sweet & Sour Chicken with Mango

This is quite a sweet dish as mango has a sweet, scented flavor.

Serves 4

INGREDIENTS

1 tbsp sunflower oil
6 skinless, boneless chicken thighs
1 ripe mango
2 cloves garlic, minced

8 oz leeks, shredded
1 cup beansprouts
$^2/_3$ cup mango juice
1 tbsp white wine vinegar

2 tbsp honey
2 tbsp tomato catsup
1 tsp cornstarch

1 Heat the sunflower oil in a large preheated wok.

2 Using a sharp knife, cut the chicken into bite-sized cubes.

3 Add the chicken to the wok and stir-fry over a high heat for 10 minutes, tossing frequently until the chicken is cooked through and golden in color.

4 Meanwhile, peel and slice the mango.

5 Add the garlic, leeks, mango, and beansprouts to the wok and stir-fry for a further 2–3 minutes, or until softened.

6 Mix together the mango juice, white wine vinegar, honey, and tomato catsup with the cornstarch in a measuring pitcher.

7 Pour the mango juice and cornstarch mixture into the wok and stir-fry for a further 2 minutes, or until the juices start to thicken.

8 Transfer to a warmed serving dish and serve immediately.

COOK'S TIP

Mango juice is available in jars from most supermarkets and is quite thick and sweet. If unavailable, paste and sieve a ripe mango and add a little water to make up the required quantity.

Stir-Fried Chicken with Lemon & Sesame Seeds

Sesame seeds have a strong flavor which adds nuttiness to recipes.
They are perfect for coating these thin chicken strips.

Serves 4

INGREDIENTS

4 boneless, skinless chicken breasts
1 egg white
2 tbsp sesame seeds
2 tbsp vegetable oil

1 onion, sliced
1 tbsp demerara sugar
finely grated peel and juice of
   1 lemon

3 tbsp lemon curd
7 oz can waterchestnuts
lemon peel, to garnish

1 Place the chicken breasts between 2 sheets of plastic wrap and pound with a rolling pin to flatten. Slice the chicken into thin strips.

2 Whisk the egg white until light and foamy.

3 Dip the chicken strips into the egg white, then into the sesame seeds until coated evenly.

4 Heat the oil in a large preheated wok.

5 Add the onion to the wok and stir-fry for 2 minutes or until just softened.

6 Add the sesame-coated chicken to the wok and continue stir-frying for 5 minutes, or until the chicken turns golden.

7 Mix together the sugar, lemon peel, lemon juice, and the lemon curd and add the mixture to the wok. Allow the lemon mixture to bubble slightly without stirring.

8 Drain the waterchestnuts and slice them thinly, using a sharp knife. Add the waterchestnuts to the wok and heat through for 2 minutes. Transfer to serving bowls, garnish with lemon peel, and serve hot.

COOK'S TIP

Waterchestnuts are commonly added to Chinese recipes for their crunchy texture as they do not have a great deal of flavor.

Honey & Soy Stir-Fried Chicken with Beansprouts

*Honey is often added to Chinese recipes for sweetness.
It combines well with the saltiness of the soy sauce.*

Serves 4

INGREDIENTS

2 tbsp honey
3 tbsp light soy sauce
1 tsp Chinese five-spice powder
1 tbsp sweet sherry
1 clove garlic, minced

8 chicken thighs
1 tbsp sunflower oil
1 red chili
$1^1/_4$ cups baby corn-on-the-cobs,
 halved

8 scallions, sliced
$1^1/_2$ cups beansprouts

1 Mix together the honey, soy sauce, Chinese five-spice powder, sherry, and garlic in a large bowl.

2 Using a sharp knife, make 3 slashes in the skin of each chicken thigh. Brush the honey and soy marinade over the chicken thighs, cover and leave to stand for at least 30 minutes.

3 Heat the oil in a large preheated wok.

4 Add the chicken to the wok and cook over a fairly high heat for 12–15 minutes, or until the chicken browns and the skin begins to crispen. Remove the chicken with a draining spoon.

5 Using a sharp knife, seed and very finely chop the chili.

6 Add the chili, corn-on-the-cobs, scallions, and beansprouts to the wok and stir-fry for 5 minutes.

7 Return the chicken to the wok and mix all of the ingredients together until completely heated through.

8 Transfer to serving plates and serve immediately.

COOK'S TIP

Chinese five-spice powder is found in most large supermarkets and is a blend of aromatic spices.

Chicken Chop Suey

Both well-known and popular, chop suey dishes are easy to make and delicious. They are based on beansprouts and soy sauce with a meat or vegetable flavoring.

Serves 4

INGREDIENTS

4 tbsp light soy sauce
2 tsp light brown sugar
1¼ lb skinless, boneless chicken
  breasts
3 tbsp vegetable oil

2 onions, quartered
2 garlic cloves, minced
12 oz beansprouts
3 tsp sesame oil

1 tbsp cornstarch
3 tbsp water
2 cups chicken stock
shredded leek, to garnish

1 Mix the soy sauce and sugar together, stirring until the sugar has dissolved.

2 Trim any fat from the chicken and cut the meat into thin strips. Place the chicken strips in a shallow glass dish and spoon the soy mixture over them, turning to coat. Leave to marinate in the refrigerator for 20 minutes.

3 Heat the oil in a preheated wok. Add the chicken and stir-fry for 2–3 minutes, until golden brown.

4 Add the onions and garlic and cook for a further 2 minutes. Add the beansprouts, cook for a further 4–5 minutes, then add the sesame oil.

5 Blend the cornstarch with the water to form a smooth paste. Pour the stock into the wok, together with the cornflour paste, and bring to a boil, stirring constantly until the sauce is thickened and clear. Transfer to a warm serving dish, garnish with shredded leek, and serve immediately.

VARIATION

This recipe may be made with strips of lean steak, pork, or with mixed vegetables. Change the type of stock accordingly.

Roasts & Casseroles

Long, slow cooking means meltingly succulent meat with a good, rich flavor. Because chicken itself does not have a strong flavor, it marries happily with almost any other ingredient, herb, or spice. The recipes in this section are drawn from many cuisines from around the world, and there are dishes from Italy, France, Hungary, the Caribbean, and from the USA. French classics include Bourguignonne of Chicken and Brittany Chicken Casserole.

The aroma of roasting chicken is always tempting and this section includes the traditional roast chicken, with all the trimmings, as well as many other imaginative treatments. Unusual stuffings to try are zucchini and lime, marmalade, or oat and herb stuffing. Many of the recipes in this section exploit the complementary flavors of chicken and fruits and there are some enticing taste combinations including cranberries, black cherries, apples, peaches, oranges, and mangoes.

Chicken with Creamy Zucchini & Lime Stuffing

A cheesy stuffing is tucked under the breast skin of the chicken to give added flavor and moistness to the meat.

Serves 6

INGREDIENTS

1 chicken, weighing 5 lb
oil for brushing
1 1/3 cups zucchini
2 tbsp butter
juice of 1 lime

STUFFING:
1/2 cup zucchini
3/4 cup medium-fat
  soft cheese
finely grated rind of 1 lime

2 tbsp fresh bread crumbs
salt and pepper

1 To make the stuffing, trim and coarsely grate the zucchini and mix with the cheese, lime peel, bread crumbs, salt, and pepper.

2 Carefully ease the skin away from the breast of the chicken.

3 Push the stuffing under the skin with your fingers, to cover the breast evenly.

4 Place the chicken in a baking pan, brush with oil, and roast in a preheated oven, 375°F, for 20 minutes per 1 lb 2 oz plus 20 minutes, or until the juices run clear when the thickest part of the chicken is pierced with a skewer.

5 Meanwhile, trim the remaining zucchini and cut into long, thin strips with a potato peeler or sharp knife. Sauté in the butter and lime juice until just tender, then serve with the chicken.

COOK'S TIP

For quicker cooking, finely grate the zucchini rather than cutting them into strips.

Boned Chicken with Parmesan

It's really very easy to bone a whole chicken, but if you prefer,
you can ask a friendly butcher to do this for you.

Serves 6

INGREDIENTS

1 chicken, weighing
    about 5 lb
8 slices Mortadella or salami
2 cups fresh white
    or brown bread crumbs

1 cup freshly grated Parmesan
    cheese
2 garlic cloves, crushed
6 tbsp chopped fresh basil
    or parsley

1 egg, beaten
pepper
fresh spring vegetables, to serve

1 Bone the chicken, keeping the skin intact. Dislocate each leg by breaking it at the thigh joint. Cut down each side of the backbone, taking care not to pierce the breast skin.

2 Pull the backbone clear of the flesh and discard. Remove the ribs, severing any attached flesh with a sharp knife.

3 Scrape the flesh from each leg and cut away the bone at the joint with a knife or shears.

4 Use the bones for stock. Lay out the boned chicken on a board, skin side down. Arrange the Mortadella slices over the chicken, overlapping slightly.

5 Put the bread crumbs, Parmesan, garlic, and basil or parsley in a bowl. Season well with pepper and mix. Stir in the beaten egg to bind the mixture together. Pile the mixture down the middle of the boned chicken, roll the meat around it, and tie securely with fine cotton string.

6 Place in a roasting dish and brush lightly with olive oil. Roast in a preheated oven at 400°F for 1½ hours or until the juices run clear when pierced.

7 Serve hot or cold, in slices, with fresh spring vegetables.

VARIATION

Replace the Mortadella with rashers
of streaky bacon, if preferred.

Breast of Chicken with York Ham & Stilton Cheese

Beet is one of the most underrated vegetables, adding flavor and color to numerous dishes. Tender young beet are used in this recipe.

Serves 4

INGREDIENTS

4 chicken suprêmes
8 fresh sage leaves
8 thin slices of York ham
2 cups Stilton cheese,
   cut into 8 slices

8 slices rindless streaky bacon
²/₃ cup chicken stock
2 tbsp port
24 shallots
1 lb 2 oz baby beet, cooked

1 tbsp cornstarch, blended with a
   little port
salt and pepper

---

1 Cut a long slit horizontally along each chicken breast to make a pocket.

2 Insert 2 sage leaves into each pocket and season lightly.

3 Wrap each slice of ham around a slice of cheese and place 2 into each chicken pocket. Carefully wrap enough bacon around each breast to completely cover the pockets containing the ham and the cheese.

4 Place the breasts in an ovenproof casserole dish and pour over the stock and port.

5 Add the shallots, cover with a lid or cooking foil and braise in a preheated oven at 375°F for about 40 minutes.

6 Carefully place each breast onto a cutting board and slice through them to create a fan effect. Serve them on a warm serving dish with the shallots and beet.

7 Put the juices from the casserole into a saucepan and bring to the boil, remove from the heat, and add the cornflour paste. Gently simmer and cook the sauce for 2 minutes, then pour over the shallots and beet.

VARIATION

Use any blue-veined cheese instead of the Stilton, if you prefer. Try Gorgonzola or Roquefort.

Pollo Catalan

The Catalan region of Spain is famous for its wonderful combinations of meat with fruit. In this recipe, peaches lend a touch of sweetness and pine nuts, cinnamon, and sherry add an unusual twist.

Serves 6

INGREDIENTS

1 cup fresh
   brown bread crumbs
$1/2$ cup pine nuts
1 small egg, beaten

4 tbsp chopped fresh thyme
   or 1 tbsp dried thyme
4 fresh peaches or
   8 canned peach halves
1 chicken, weighing about
   $5^1/2$ lb

1 tsp ground cinnamon
$3/4$ cup Amontillado sherry
4 tbsp heavy cream
salt and pepper

1 Combine the bread crumbs with ¼ cup pine nuts, the egg, and the thyme.

2 Halve and stone the peaches, removing the skin if necessary. Dice one peach into small pieces and stir into the bread crumb mixture. Season well. Spoon the stuffing into the neck cavity of the chicken, securing the skin firmly over it.

3 Place the chicken in a roasting pan. Sprinkle the cinnamon over the skin.

4 Cover loosely with foil and roast in a preheated oven, 375°F, for 1 hour, basting occasionally.

5 Remove the foil and spoon the sherry over the chicken. Cook for a further 30 minutes, basting with the sherry, until the juices run clear when the chicken is pierced in the thickest part with a skewer.

6 Sprinkle the remaining pine nuts over the remaining peach halves and place in an ovenproof

dish in the oven for the final 10 minutes of cooking time.

7 Lift the chicken on to a serving plate and arrange the peach halves around it. Skim any fat from the juices, stir in the cream, and heat gently. Serve with the chicken.

COOK'S TIP

Canned apricot halves in natural juice make an easy store-cupboard alternative.

Golden Chicken with Mango & Cranberries

This recipe, which uses a partly-boned chicken is easy to slice and serve. If you prefer, stuff in the traditional way at the neck end, and cook any remaining stuffing separately.

Serves 4

INGREDIENTS

1 chicken, weighing about 5 lb
6 slices smoked bacon

STUFFING:
1 ripe mango, diced
1/4 cup fresh or frozen cranberries
2 cups bread crumbs

1/2 tsp ground mace
1 egg, beaten
salt and pepper

GLAZE:
1/2 tsp ground turmeric
2 tsp honey
2 tsp sunflower oil

1 To part-bone the chicken, dislocate the legs and place the chicken breast-side downward. Cut a straight line through the skin along the ridge of the back. Scrape the meat down from the bone on both sides.

2 When you reach the point where the legs and wings join the body, cut through the joints. Work around the ribcage until the carcass can be lifted away.

3 Make six bacon rolls. For the stuffing, mix the mango with the cranberries, bread crumbs, and mace, then bind with egg. Season.

4 Place the chicken, skin-side down, and spoon over half the stuffing. Arrange the bacon rolls down the center, then top with the remaining stuffing. Fold the skin over and tie with string. Turn the chicken over, truss the legs, and tuck the wings underneath. Place

in a roasting pan. To make the glaze, mix the turmeric, honey, and oil, and brush over the skin.

5 Roast in a preheated oven, 375°F, for 1½–2 hours or until the juices run clear, not pink, when the chicken is pierced with a skewer. When the chicken starts to brown, cover loosely with foil to prevent overbrowning. Serve the chicken hot with vegetables.

Chicken with Marmalade Stuffing

Marmalade lovers will enjoy this festive recipe. You can use any favorite marmalade, such as lemon or grapefruit.

Serves 6

INGREDIENTS

1 chicken, weighing about 5 lb
bay leaves

STUFFING:
1 stalk celery, chopped finely
1 small onion, chopped finely
1 tbsp sunflower oil

2 cups fresh whole wheat bread
  crumbs
4 tbsp marmalade
2 tbsp chopped fresh parsley
1 egg, beaten
salt and pepper

SAUCE:
2 tsp cornstarch
2 tbsp orange juice
3 tbsp marmalade
$^2/_3$ cup chicken stock
1 medium orange
2 tbsp brandy

1 Lift the neck flap of the chicken and remove the wishbone using a small, sharp knife. Place a sprig of bay leaves inside the body cavity.

2 For the stuffing, sauté the celery and onion in the oil to soften. Add the bread crumbs, 3 tablespoons of marmalade, parsley, and egg. Season and use to stuff the neck cavity of the chicken. Any extra stuffing may be cooked separately.

3 Place the chicken in a roasting pan and brush lightly with oil. Roast in a preheated oven, 375°F, for 20 minutes per 1 lb 2 oz plus 20 minutes or until the juices run clear when the chicken is pierced in the thickest part with a skewer. Remove from the oven and glaze with the remaining marmalade.

4 Meanwhile, to make the sauce, blend the cornstarch in a pan with the orange juice, then add the marmalade and chicken stock. Heat gently, stirring, until thickened and smooth. Remove from the heat. Cut the segments from the orange, discarding all white pith and membrane. Just before serving, add the orange segments and brandy to the sauce and bring to the boil.

5 Serve the chicken with the orange sauce, any extra stuffing, and new potatoes.

Feta Chicken with Mountain Herbs

Chicken goes well with most savory herbs, especially during the summer, when fresh herbs are at their best. This combination makes a good partner for tangy feta cheese and sun-ripened tomatoes.

Serves 4

INGREDIENTS

8 skinless, boneless chicken thighs
2 tbsp each chopped fresh thyme,
  rosemary and oregano
4$^{1}/_{2}$ oz feta cheese
1 tbsp milk
2 tbsp all-purpose flour
salt and pepper

thyme, rosemary, and oregano,
  to garnish

TOMATO SAUCE:
1 medium onion, roughly chopped
1 garlic clove, crushed
1 tbsp olive oil

4 medium plum tomatoes, quartered
sprig each of thyme, rosemary,
  and oregano

1 Spread out the chicken thighs, smooth side downward.

2 Divide the herbs among the chicken thighs, then cut the cheese into eight sticks. Place one stick of cheese in the center of each chicken thigh. Season well, then roll up to enclose the cheese.

3 Place the rolls in an ovenproof dish, brush with milk, and dust with flour to coat.

4 Bake in a preheated oven, 375°F, for 25–30 minutes, or until golden brown. The juices should run clear and not pink when the chicken is pierced with a skewer in the thickest part.

5 To make the sauce, cook the onion and garlic in the olive oil, stirring, until softened and starting to brown.

6 Add the tomatoes, reduce the heat, cover, and simmer for 15–20 minutes or until soft.

7 Add the herbs, then transfer to a food processor and blend to a paste. Press through a strainer to make a smooth, rich sauce. Season and serve the sauce with the chicken, garnished with herbs.

Festive Apple Chicken

The richly flavored stuffing in this recipe is cooked under the breast skin of the chicken, so not only is all the flavor sealed in, but the chicken stays really moist and succulent during cooking.

Serves 6

INGREDIENTS

1 chicken, weighing 4 lb
2 eating apples
1 tbsp butter
1 tbsp redcurrant jelly
mixed vegetables, to serve

STUFFING:
1 tbsp butter
1 small onion, chopped finely
2 oz mushrooms, chopped finely
2 oz smoked ham,
   chopped finely

$^{1}/_{2}$ cup fresh bread crumbs
1 tbsp chopped fresh parsley
1 crisp eating apple
1 tbsp lemon juice
oil, for brushing
salt and pepper

1 To make the stuffing, melt the butter and fry the onion gently, stirring until softened but not browned. Stir in the mushrooms and cook for 2–3 minutes. Remove from the heat and stir in the ham, bread crumbs, and the chopped parsley.

2 Core the apple, leaving the skin on, and grate coarsely. Add the stuffing mixture to the apple with the lemon juice. Season to taste.

3 Loosen the breast skin of the chicken and carefully spoon the stuffing mixture under it, smoothing the skin over evenly with your hands.

4 Place the chicken in a roasting pan and brush lightly with oil.

5 Roast the chicken in a preheated oven, 375°F, for 25 minutes per 1 lb plus 25 minutes, or until there is no trace of pink in the juices when the chicken is

pierced through the thickest part with a skewer. If the breast starts to brown too much, cover the chicken with foil.

6 Core and slice the remaining apples and sauté in the butter until golden. Stir in the redcurrant jelly and warm through until melted. Garnish the chicken with the apple slices and serve with mixed vegetables.

Whiskey Roast Chicken

An unusual change from a plain roast, with a distinctly warming Scottish flavor and a delicious oatmeal stuffing.

Serves 6

INGREDIENTS

1 chicken, weighing 4 lb 8 oz
oil, for brushing
1 tbsp heather honey
2 tbsp Scotch whiskey
2 tbsp all-purpose flour
1¼ cups chicken stock

STUFFING:
1 medium onion, finely chopped
1 stalk celery, sliced thinly
1 tbsp butter or sunflower oil
1 tsp dried thyme
4 tbsp porridge oats

4 tbsp chicken stock
salt and pepper
a green vegetable and sautéed
    potatoes, to serve

1 To make the stuffing, fry the onion and celery in the butter or oil, stirring over a medium heat until softened.

2 Remove from the heat and stir in the thyme, oats, stock, salt, and pepper.

3 Stuff the neck end of the chicken with the mixture and tuck the neck flap under. Place in a roasting pan, brush lightly with oil, and roast in a preheated oven, 375°F, for about 1 hour.

4 Mix the heather honey with 1 tablespoon whiskey and brush the mixture over the chicken. Return to the oven for a further 20 minutes, or until the chicken is golden brown and the juices run clear when the chicken is pierced through the thickest part with a skewer.

5 Lift the chicken on to a serving plate. Skim the fat from the juices then stir in the flour. Stir over a moderate heat until the mixture starts to bubble, then gradually add the stock and remaining whiskey.

6 Bring to the boil, stirring, simmer for 1 minute, and serve the chicken with the sauce, a green vegetable, and sautéed potatoes.

Cheddar Baked Chicken

Cheese and mustard, and a simple, crispy coating, make a delicious combination for this healthy dish.

Serves 4

INGREDIENTS

1 tbsp milk

2 tbsp prepared English mustard

1 cup grated mature
   hard cheese

3 tbsp all-purpose flour

2 tbsp chopped fresh chives

4 skinless, boneless chicken breasts

1 Mix together the milk and mustard in a bowl. In another bowl, combine the cheese, flour, and chives.

2 Dip the chicken into the milk and mustard mixture, brushing to coat evenly.

3 Dip the chicken breasts into the cheese mixture, pressing to coat evenly. Place on a cookie sheet and spoon any spare cheese coating over the top.

4 Bake in a preheated oven, 400°F, for 30–35 minutes, or until golden brown and the juices run clear, not pink, when pierced with a skewer. Serve the chicken hot, with jacket potatoes and fresh vegetables, or serve cold, with a crisp salad.

COOK'S TIP

There are several varieties of mustard available. For a sharper flavor try French varieties – Meaux mustard has a grainy texture with a warm, spicy flavor while Dijon mustard is medium-hot and tangy.

COOK'S TIP

It is a good idea to freeze herbs as they retain their color, flavor, and nutrients very well. Chives are particularly suitable for freezing – store them in labeled plastic bags and shake them dry before use. Dried chives are not an adequate substitute for fresh.

Honey & Mustard Baked Chicken

Chicken portions are brushed with a classic combination of honey and mustard then a crunchy coating of poppy seeds is added.

Serves 4–6

INGREDIENTS

8 chicken portions
4 tbsp butter, melted
4 tbsp mild mustard
4 tbsp honey
2 tbsp lemon juice
1 tsp paprika

3 tbsp poppy seeds
salt and pepper
tomato and corn salad,
   to serve

1 Place the chicken pieces, skinless side down, on a large cookie sheet.

2 Place all the ingredients except the poppy seeds into a large bowl and blend together thoroughly.

3 Brush the mixture over the chicken portions.

4 Bake in the center of a preheated oven, 400°F, for 15 minutes.

5 Carefully turn over the chicken pieces and coat the top side of the chicken with the remaining honey and mustard mixture.

6 Sprinkle the chicken with poppy seeds and return to the oven for a further 15 minutes.

7 Arrange the chicken on a serving dish, pour over the cooking juices, and serve with a tomato and corn salad, if wished.

COOK'S TIP

Mexican rice makes an excellent accompaniment to this dish: boil the rice for 10 minutes, drain, then fry for 5 minutes. Add chopped onions, garlic, tomatoes, carrots, and chili, and cook for 1 minute before adding stock. Bring to the boil, cover and simmer for 20 minutes, adding more stock if necessary. Add peas 5 minutes before the end of the cooking time.

Country Chicken Bake

This economical bake is a complete meal – its crusty, herb-flavored French bread topping mops up the tasty juices, and means there's no need to serve potatoes or rice separately.

Serves 4

INGREDIENTS

2 tbsp sunflower oil

4 chicken quarters

16 small whole onions, peeled

3 stalks celery, sliced

14 oz can red kidney beans

4 medium tomatoes, quartered

scant 1 cup dry cider or stock

4 tbsp chopped fresh parsley

1 tsp paprika

4 tbsp butter

12 slices French bread

salt and pepper

1 Heat the oil in a flameproof casserole and fry the chicken quarters two at a time until golden. Using a draining spoon, remove the chicken from the pan and set aside until required.

2 Add the onions and fry, turning occasionally, until golden brown. Add the celery and fry for 2–3 minutes. Return the chicken to the pan, then stir in the beans, tomatoes, cider, half the parsley, salt, and pepper. Sprinkle with the paprika.

3 Cover and cook in a preheated oven, 400°F, for 20–25 minutes, until the chicken juices run clear when pierced with a skewer.

4 Mix the remaining parsley with the butter and spread evenly over the French bread.

5 Uncover the casserole, arrange the bread slices so that they are overlapping on top and bake for a further 10–12 minutes, until golden and crisp.

COOK'S TIP

Add a minced garlic clove to the parsley butter for extra flavor.

VARIATION

For a more unusual Italian-tasting dish, replace the garlic and parsley bread topping with the pesto-covered toasts.

Country Chicken Hotch-potch

There are many regional versions of hotch-potch, all using fresh, local ingredients. Now, there are an endless variety of ingredients available all year, perfect for traditional one-pot cooking.

Serves 4

INGREDIENTS

4 chicken quarters
6 medium potatoes, cut
  into $1/4$ inch slices
2 sprigs thyme

2 sprigs rosemary
2 bay leaves
1 cup rindless, smoked streaky bacon,
  diced
1 large onion, chopped finely

1 cup sliced carrots
$2/3$ cup stout
2 tbsp melted butter
salt and pepper

1 Remove the skin from the chicken quarters, if preferred.

2 Arrange a layer of potato slices in the bottom of a wide casserole. Season with salt and pepper, then add the thyme, rosemary, and bay leaves.

3 Top with the chicken quarters, then sprinkle with the diced bacon, onion, and carrots. Season well and arrange the remaining potato slices on top, overlapping slightly.

4 Pour over the stout, brush the potatoes with the melted butter, and cover with a lid.

5 Bake in a preheated oven, 300°F, for about 2 hours, uncovering for the last 30 minutes to allow the potatoes to brown. Serve hot.

COOK'S TIP

Serve the hotch-potch with dumplings for a truly hearty meal.

VARIATION

This dish is also delicious with stewing lamb, cut into chunks. You can add different vegetables depending on what is in season – try leeks and swedes for a slightly sweeter flavor.

Jamaican Hotch-Potch

A tasty way to make chicken joints go a long way, this hearty casserole, spiced with the warm, subtle flavor of ginger, is a good choice for a Halloween party.

Serves 4

INGREDIENTS

2 tsp sunflower oil
4 chicken drumsticks
4 chicken thighs
1 medium onion
1 lb 10 oz piece squash
  or pumpkin, diced

1 green bell pepper, sliced
1 inch fresh gingerroot,
  chopped finely
14 oz can chopped tomatoes
1¼ cups chicken stock
¼ cup split lentils

garlic salt and cayenne pepper
2 oz can corn-on-the-cob
crusty bread, to serve

---

1 Heat the oil in a large flameproof casserole and fry the chicken joints until golden, turning frequently.

2 Using a sharp knife, peel and slice the onion, peel and dice the pumpkin or squash, and seed and slice the bell pepper.

3 Drain any excess fat from the pan and add the prepared onion, pumpkin, and pepper. Gently fry for a few minutes until lightly browned. Add the chopped ginger, tomatoes, chicken stock, and lentils. Season lightly with garlic salt and cayenne pepper.

4 Cover the casserole and place in a preheated oven, 375°F, for about 1 hour, until the vegetables are tender and the chicken juices run clear if pierced with a skewer.

5 Add the drained corn and cook for a further 5 minutes. Season to taste and serve with crusty bread.

VARIATION

If you can't find fresh gingerroot, add 1 teaspoon allspice for a warm, fragrant aroma.

VARIATION

If squash or pumpkin is not available, rutabaga makes a good substitute.

Chicken Madeira French-Style

Madeira is a fortified wine which can be used in both sweet and savory dishes.
Here it adds a rich, full flavor to the casserole.

Serves 8

INGREDIENTS

2 tbsp butter
20 baby onions
$1^1/_2$ cups carrots, sliced
$1^1/_2$ cups bacon, chopped
3 cups button mushrooms

1 chicken, weighing about 3 lb 5 oz
$1^7/_8$ cups white wine
$^1/_4$ cup seasoned flour
$1^7/_8$ cups chicken stock
bouquet garni

$^2/_3$ cup Madeira wine
salt and pepper
mashed potato or pasta, to serve

1 Heat the butter in a large skillet and fry the onions, carrots, bacon, and button mushrooms for 3 minutes, stirring frequently. Transfer to a large casserole dish.

2 Add the chicken to the skillet and brown all over. Transfer to the casserole dish with the vegetables and bacon.

3 Add the white wine and cook until the wine is nearly completely reduced.

4 Sprinkle with the seasoned flour, stirring to avoid lumps from forming.

5 Add the chicken stock, salt, and pepper to taste and the bouquet garni. Cover and cook the casserole for 2 hours. About 30 minutes before the end of cooking time, add the Madeira wine and continue cooking uncovered.

6 Carve the chicken and serve with mashed potato or pasta.

COOK'S TIP

You can add any combination of herbs to this recipe – chervil is a popular herb in French cuisine, but add it at the end of cooking so that its delicate flavor is not lost. Other herbs that work well with chicken are parsley and tarragon.

Gardener's Chicken

Any combination of small, young vegetables can be roasted with the chicken, such as zucchini, leeks, and onions.

Serves 4

INGREDIENTS

4 cups parsnips, peeled and chopped
³/4 cup carrots, peeled and chopped
¹/2 cup fresh bread crumbs
¹/4 tsp grated nutmeg
1 tbsp chopped fresh parsley
3 lb 5 oz chicken

bunch parsley
¹/2 onion
2 tbsp butter, softened
4 tbsp olive oil
1 lb 2 oz new potatoes, scrubbed

1 lb 2 oz baby carrots
washed and trimmed
salt and pepper
chopped fresh parsley, to garnish

1 To make the stuffing, put the parsnips and carrots into a pan, half cover with water, and bring to the boil. Cover the pan and simmer until tender. Drain well then paste in a blender or food processor. Transfer the paste to a bowl and leave to cool.

2 Mix in the bread crumbs, nutmeg, and parsley and season with salt and pepper.

3 Put the stuffing into the neck end of the chicken and push a little under the skin over the breast meat. Secure the flap of skin with a small metal skewer or toothpick.

4 Place the bunch of parsley and onion inside the cavity of the chicken, then place the chicken in a large roasting pan.

5 Spread the butter over the skin and season with salt and pepper, cover with foil, and place in a preheated oven, 375°F, for 30 minutes.

6 Meanwhile, heat the oil in a skillet and lightly brown the potatoes.

7 Transfer the potatoes to the roasting pan and add the baby carrots. Baste the chicken and continue to cook for a further hour, basting the chicken and vegetables after 30 minutes. Remove the foil for the last 20 minutes to allow the skin to crisp. Garnish the vegetables with chopped parsley and serve.

Mediterranean-Style Sunday Roast

A roast that is full of Mediterranean flavor. A mixture of feta cheese, rosemary and sun-dried tomatoes is stuffed under the chicken skin, then roasted with garlic, new potatoes, and vegetables.

Serves 6

INGREDIENTS

5 lb 8 oz chicken

sprigs of fresh rosemary

$^3/_4$ cup feta cheese,
coarsely grated

2 tbsp sun-dried tomato paste

4 tbsp butter, softened

1 bulb garlic

2 lb 4 oz new potatoes, halved
if large

1 each red, green, and yellow
bell pepper, cut into chunks

3 zucchini, sliced thinly

2 tbsp olive oil

2 tbsp all-purpose flour

2$^1/_2$ cups chicken stock

salt and pepper

1 Rinse the chicken inside and out with cold water and drain well. Carefully cut between the skin and the top of the breast meat using a small pointed knife. Slide a finger into the slit and carefully enlarge it to form a pocket. Continue until the skin is completely lifted away from both breasts and the top of the legs.

2 Chop the leaves from 3 rosemary stems. Mix with the feta, sun-dried tomato paste, butter, and pepper then spoon under the skin. Put the chicken in a large roasting pan, cover with foil, and cook in a preheated oven, 375°F, for 20 minutes per 1 lb 2 oz plus 20 minutes.

3 Break the garlic bulb into cloves but do not peel. Add the vegetables to the chicken after 40 minutes.

4 Drizzle with oil, tuck in a few stems of rosemary, and season well. Cook for the remaining time, removing the foil for the last 40 minutes of cooking to brown the chicken.

5 Transfer the chicken to a serving platter. Place some of the vegetables around the chicken and transfer the remainder to a warmed serving dish. Pour the fat out of the roasting pan and stir the flour into the remaining pan juices. Cook for 2 minutes then gradually stir in the stock. Bring to the boil, stirring until thickened. Strain into a sauce boat and serve with the chicken.

Pot Roast Orange & Sesame Chicken

This colorful, nutritious pot-roast could be served for a family meal or for a special dinner.
Add more vegetables if you're feeding a crowd – if your roasting pot is large enough!

Serves 4

INGREDIENTS

2 tbsp sunflower oil
1 chicken, weighing about
　3 lb 5 oz
2 large oranges
2 small onions, quartered

2 cups small whole
　carrots or thin carrots, cut
　into 2 inch pieces
$^2/_3$ cup orange juice
2 tbsp brandy

2 tbsp sesame seeds
1 tbsp cornstarch
salt and pepper

1　Heat the oil in a large flameproof casserole and fry the chicken, turning occasionally until evenly browned.

2　Cut one orange in half and place half inside the chicken cavity. Place the chicken in a large, deep casserole. Arrange the onions and carrots around the chicken.

3　Season well and pour over the orange juice.

4　Cut the remaining oranges into thin wedges and tuck around the chicken in the casserole, among the vegetables.

5　Cover and cook in a preheated oven, 350°F, for about 1½ hours, or until there is no trace of pink in the chicken juices when pierced, and the vegetables are tender. Remove the lid and sprinkle with the brandy and sesame seeds, and return to the oven for 10 minutes.

6　To serve, lift the chicken onto a large platter. Place the vegetables around the chicken.

Skim any excess fat from the juices. Blend the cornflour with 1 tablespoon cold water, stir into the juices, and bring to the boil, stirring all the time. Adjust the seasoning to taste, then serve the sauce with the chicken.

VARIATION

Use lemons instead of oranges for a sharper citrus flavor and place a sprig of fresh thyme in the chicken cavity with the lemon half as they are a good flavor combination.

Springtime Roast Chicken

Baby chickens are simple to prepare, take about 30 minutes to roast and can be easily cut in half lengthways with a sharp knife. One baby chicken makes a substantial serving for each person.

Serves 4

INGREDIENTS

5 tbsp fresh brown bread crumbs
$1/2$ cup fromage blanc
   or low-fat crème fraîche
5 tbsp chopped fresh parsley
5 tbsp chopped fresh chives
4 baby chickens
1 tbsp sunflower oil

$1^1/2$ lb young spring
   vegetables such as carrots,
   zucchini, sugar snap
   peas, corn-on-the-cob,
   and turnips, cut into small chunks
$1/2$ cup boiling chicken stock
2 tsp cornstarch

$2/3$ cup dry white wine
salt and pepper

1 In a bowl, mix together the bread crumbs, one-third of the fromage blanc or low-fat crème fraîche and 2 tablespoons each of parsley and chives. Season well with salt and pepper then spoon into the neck ends of the baby chickens. Place the chickens on a rack in a roasting pan, brush with oil, and season well.

2 Roast in a preheated oven, 425°F, for 30–35 minutes or until the juices run clear, not pink, when the chickens are pierced with a skewer.

3 Place the vegetables in a shallow ovenproof dish in one layer and add half the remaining herbs with the chicken stock. Cover and bake for 25–30 minutes until tender. Strain the vegetables, reserving the cooking juices, and keep warm.

4 Lift the chickens onto a serving plate and skim any fat from the juices in the pan. Add the reserved vegetable juices.

5 Blend the cornstarch with the wine and whisk into the sauce with the remaining fromage blanc or low-fat crème fraîche. Whisk until boiling, then add the remaining herbs. Season to taste. Spoon the sauce over the chickens and serve with the vegetables.

Honeyed Citrus Chicken

This fat-free recipe is great for summer entertaining served simply with a green salad and new potatoes. If you cut the chicken in half and press it flat, you can roast it in under an hour.

Serves 4

INGREDIENTS

4 lb 8 oz chicken
salt and pepper
tarragon sprigs, to garnish

MARINADE:
1¹/₄ cups orange juice
3 tbsp cider vinegar
3 tbsp honey

2 tbsp chopped fresh tarragon
2 oranges, cut into wedges

SAUCE:
handful of tarragon sprigs, chopped
1 cup fat-free fromage blanc
2 tbsp orange juice

1 tsp honey
¹/₂ cup stuffed olives, chopped

1 Put the chicken on a chopping board with the breast downward. Cut through the bottom part of the carcass using poultry shears or heavy kitchen scissors, making sure not to cut right through to the breast bone below.

2 Rinse the chicken with cold water, drain, and place on a board with the skin side uppermost. Press the chicken flat, then cut off the leg ends.

3 Thread two long wooden skewers through the bird to keep it flat. Season the skin.

4 Put all the marinade ingredients, except the orange wedges, in a shallow, nonmetallic dish. Mix, then add the chicken. Cover and chill for 4 hours, turning the chicken several times.

5 To make the sauce, mix all the ingredients and season. Spoon into a serving dish, cover, and chill.

6 Transfer the chicken and marinade to a roasting pan, open out the chicken, and place skin-side downward. Tuck the orange wedges around the chicken and roast in a preheated oven, 400°F, for 25 minutes. Turn the chicken over and roast for another 20–30 minutes. Baste until the chicken is browned and the juices run clear when pierced with a skewer. Garnish with tarragon and serve with the sauce.

Poussin with Dried Fruits

Baby chickens are ideal for a one or two portion meal, and cook very easily and quickly for a special dinner. If you're cooking for one, a microwave makes cooking even quicker and more convenient.

Serves 2

INGREDIENTS

³/₄ cup dried apples,
   peaches, and prunes
¹/₂ cup boiling water
2 baby chickens
¹/₃ cup walnut halves

1 tbsp honey
1 tsp ground allspice
1 tbsp walnut oil

salt and pepper
fresh vegetables and new potatoes,
   to serve

1 Place the dried fruits in a bowl, cover with the boiling water, and leave to stand for about 30 minutes.

2 Cut the chickens in half down the breastbone using a sharp knife, or leave them whole, if you prefer.

3 Mix the fruit and any juices remaining in the bowl with the walnut halves, honey, and ground allspice and divide the mixture between two small roasting bags or squares of foil.

4 Brush the chickens with walnut oil and sprinkle with salt and pepper then place on top of the fruits.

5 Close the roasting bags or fold the foil over to enclose the chickens and bake on a cookie sheet in a preheated oven, 375°F, for 25–30 minutes or until the juices run clear and not pink when the chicken is pierced in the thickest part with a skewer. To cook in a microwave, use microwave roasting bags and cook on high power for 6–7 minutes.

6 Serve hot with fresh vegetables and new potatoes.

COOK'S TIP

Alternative dried fruits that can be used in this recipe are cherries, mangoes, or papaya.

Roast Chicken with Cilantro & Garlic

This recipe for chicken is coated with a fresh-flavored marinade then roasted.
Try serving it with rice, yogurt, and salad.

Serves 4–6

INGREDIENTS

3 sprigs fresh cilantro, chopped
4 garlic cloves
$^1/_2$ tsp salt
1 tsp pepper

4 tbsp lemon juice
4 tbsp olive oil
1 large chicken
pepper

sprig of fresh parsley, to garnish
boiled potatoes and carrots, to serve

1 Place the chopped cilantro, garlic, salt, pepper, lemon juice, and olive oil in a pestle and mortar and pound together or blend in a food processor. Chill for 4 hours to allow the flavors to develop.

2 Place the chicken in a roasting pan. Coat generously with the cilantro and garlic mixture.

3 Sprinkle with pepper and roast in a preheated oven,

375°F, on a low shelf for 1½ hours, basting every 20 minutes with the coriander mixture. If the chicken starts to turn brown, cover with foil. Garnish with parsley and serve with the potatoes and carrots.

COOK'S TIP

For pounding small quantities it is best to use a pestle and mortar so as little as possible of the mixture is left in the container.

VARIATION

Any fresh herb can be used in this recipe instead of the cilantro. Tarragon or thyme are a good combination with chicken.

Roast Chicken Breasts with Bacon & Dripping Triangles

Chicken suprêmes have a little bit of the wing bone remaining which makes them easy to pick up and eat. In this recipe, a tart, fruity sauce perfectly complements the chicken and dripping triangles.

Serves 8

INGREDIENTS

.4 tbsp butter
juice of 1 lemon
1 cup redcurrants or cranberries
1–2 tbsp muscovado sugar

8 chicken suprêmes or breasts
16 slices of streaky bacon
thyme
4 tbsp beef dripping

4 slices of bread, cut into triangles
salt and pepper

1 Heat the butter in a saucepan, add the lemon juice, redcurrants or cranberries, muscovado sugar, and salt and pepper to taste. Cook for 1 minute and allow to cool until required.

2 Meanwhile, season the chicken with salt and pepper. Wrap 2 slices of streaky bacon around each breast and sprinkle with thyme.

3 Wrap each breast in a piece of lightly greased foil and place in a roasting pan. Roast in a preheated oven, 400°F, for 15 minutes. Remove the foil and roast for another 10 minutes.

4 Heat the dripping in a skillet, add the bread triangles and fry on both sides until golden brown.

5 Arrange the triangles on a large serving plate and top each with a chicken breast. Serve with a spoonful of the fruit sauce.

COOK'S TIP

You can use either chopped fresh thyme or dried thyme in this recipe, but remember that dried herbs have a stronger flavor so you only need half the quantity compared to fresh herbs.

Roast Chicken in Wild Mushroom Sauce

This unusual chicken dish has the flavor of roast chicken but is finished off in a casserole with a wild mushroom sauce.

Serves 4

INGREDIENTS

$^1/_3$ cup butter, softened
1 garlic clove, crushed
1 large chicken
$2^1/_4$ cups wild mushrooms
12 shallots
2 tbsp all-purpose flour

$^2/_3$ cup brandy
$1^1/_4$ cups heavy cream
salt and pepper
1 tbsp chopped fresh parsley, to garnish

wild rice or roast potatoes, and green beans, to serve

1 Place the butter, garlic, and salt and pepper in a bowl and combine well.

2 Rub the mixture inside and outside of the chicken and leave for 2 hours.

3 Place the chicken in a large roasting pan and roast in the center of a preheated oven, 450°F, for 1½ hours, basting with garlic butter every ten minutes.

4 Remove the chicken from the roasting pan and set aside to cool slightly.

5 Transfer the chicken juices to a saucepan and cook the mushrooms and shallots for 5 minutes. Sprinkle with the flour. Add the warm brandy and ignite using a taper or long match.

6 Add the heavy cream and cook for 3 minutes on a very low heat, stirring all the time.

7 Remove the bones and cut the chicken into small bite-sized pieces, then place the meat in a casserole dish. Cover with the mushroom sauce and bake in the oven, with the heat reduced to 325°F for a further 12 minutes. Garnish with the parsley and serve with wild rice or roast potatoes and green beans.

Rich Mediterranean Chicken Casserole

A colorful casserole packed with sunshine flavors from the Mediterranean.
Sun-dried tomatoes add a wonderful richness and you need very few to make this dish really special.

Serves 4

INGREDIENTS

8 chicken thighs
2 tbsp olive oil
1 medium red onion, sliced
2 garlic cloves, crushed
1 large red bell pepper, sliced thickly
thinly pared rind and juice
   of 1 small orange

½ cup chicken stock
14 oz can chopped tomatoes
½ cup sun-dried
   tomatoes, thinly sliced
1 tbsp chopped fresh thyme
½ cup pitted black olives
salt and pepper

thyme sprigs and orange
   peel, to garnish
crusty fresh bread, to serve

1 In a heavy or non-stick large skillet, fry the chicken without fat over a fairly high heat, turning occasionally until golden brown. Using a draining spoon, drain off any excess fat from the chicken and transfer to a flameproof casserole.

2 Fry the onion, garlic, and bell pepper in the pan over a moderate heat for 3–4 minutes. Transfer to the casserole.

3 Add the orange peel and juice, chicken stock, canned tomatoes, and sun-dried tomatoes and stir to combine.

4 Bring to the boil then cover the casserole with a lid and simmer very gently over a low heat for about 1 hour, stirring occasionally. Add the chopped fresh thyme and pitted black olives, then adjust the seasoning with salt and pepper.

5 Scatter orange peel and thyme over the casserole to garnish, and serve with crusty bread.

COOK'S TIP

Sun-dried tomatoes have a dense texture and concentrated taste, and add intense flavor to slow-cooking casseroles.

Brittany Chicken Casserole

A hearty, one-dish meal that would make a substantial lunch or supper. As it requires a long cooking time, make double quantities and freeze half to eat later.

Serves 6

INGREDIENTS

2^1/$_2$ cups beans, such as flageolets, soaked overnight and drained
2 tbsp butter
2 tbsp olive oil
3 rindless bacon slices, chopped

1^3/$_4$ lb chicken pieces
1 tbsp all-purpose flour
1^1/$_4$ cups cider
^{2}/$_3$ cup chicken stock
14 shallots

2 tbsp honey, warmed
8 oz ready-cooked beet
salt and pepper

1 Cook the chosen beans in salted boiling water for about 25 minutes.

2 Heat the butter and olive oil in a flameproof casserole, add the bacon and chicken, and cook for 5 minutes.

3 Sprinkle with the flour then add the cider and chicken stock, stirring constantly to avoid lumps forming. Season with salt and pepper to taste and bring to the boil.

4 Add the beans then cover the casserole tightly with a lid or cooking foil and bake in the center of a preheated oven, 1325°F, for 2 hours.

5 About 15 minutes before the end of cooking time, remove the lid or cooking foil from the casserole.

6 In a skillet, gently cook the shallots and honey together for 5 minutes, turning the shallots frequently.

7 Add the shallots and cooked beet to the casserole and leave to finish cooking in the oven for the last 15 minutes.

COOK'S TIP

To save time, use canned flageolet beans instead of dried. Drain and rinse before adding to the chicken.

Old English Chicken Stewed in Ale

This is a slow-cooked, old-fashioned stew to warm up a wintery day. The rarebit toasts are a perfect accompaniment to soak up the rich juices, but if you prefer, serve the stew with jacket potatoes.

Serves 4-6

INGREDIENTS

4 large, skinless chicken thighs
2 tbsp all-purpose flour
2 tbsp English mustard powder
2 tbsp sunflower oil
1 tbsp butter
4 small onions
2¹/₂ cups beer

2 tbsp Worcestershire sauce
3 tbsp chopped fresh sage leaves
salt and pepper

RAREBIT TOASTS:
¹/₂ cup grated hard
   English Cheddar

1 tsp English mustard powder
1 tsp all-purpose flour
1 tsp Worcestershire sauce
1 tbsp beer
2 slices whole wheat toast

1 Trim any excess fat from the chicken and toss in the flour and mustard powder to coat evenly. Heat the sunflower oil and butter in a large flameproof casserole and fry the chicken over a fairly high heat, turning occasionally, until golden. Remove the chicken from the casserole with a draining spoon and keep hot.

2 Peel the onions and slice into wedges, then fry quickly until golden. Add the chicken, beer, Worcestershire sauce, fresh sage, and salt and pepper to taste. Bring to the boil, cover, and simmer very gently for about 1½ hours, until the chicken is very tender.

3 Meanwhile, make the rarebit toasts: mix the cheese with the mustard powder, flour, Worcestershire sauce, and beer. Spread the mixture over the toasts and cook under a hot broiler for about 1 minute, until melted and golden. Cut into triangles.

4 Stir the sage leaves into the chicken stew, bring to the boil, and serve with the rarebit toasts, a green vegetable and new

COOK'S TIP

If you do not have fresh sage, use 2 tsp of dried sage in step 2.

Garlic Chicken Casserole

This is a cassoulet with a twist – it is made with chicken instead of duck and lamb. Save time by using canned beans, such as borlotti or cannellini beans, which are both good in this dish.

Serves 4

INGREDIENTS

4 tbsp sunflower oil
1³/4 lb chicken meat, chopped
3 cups mushrooms, sliced
16 shallots
6 garlic cloves, minced
1 tbsp all-purpose flour

1 cup white wine
1 cup chicken stock
1 bouquet garni (1 bay leaf, sprig
thyme, celery, parsley, and sage
tied together with string)
14 oz can borlotti beans

salt and pepper
patty pans, to serve

---

1 Heat the sunflower oil in an ovenproof casserole and fry the chicken until browned all over. Remove the chicken from the casserole with a draining spoon and set aside until required.

2 Add the mushrooms, shallots, and garlic to the fat in the casserole and cook for 4 minutes.

3 Return the chicken to the casserole and sprinkle with the flour, then cook for a further 2 minutes.

4 Add the white wine and chicken stock, stir until boiling, then add the bouquet garni. Season well with salt and pepper.

5 Drain the borlotti beans and rinse thoroughly, then add to the casserole.

6 Cover and place in the center of a preheated oven, 300°F, for 2 hours. Remove the bouquet garni and serve the casserole with patty pans.

COOK'S TIP

Mushrooms are ideal in a low-fat diet because they are high in flavor and contain no fat. Experiment with the wealth of varieties that are now available from supermarkets.

COOK'S TIP

Serve the casserole with whole wheat rice to make this filling dish go even further.

Chicken with Shallots in Wild Mushroom & Ginger Sauce

This recipe has an oriental flavor, which can be further enhanced with chopped scallions, cinnamon, and lemongrass.

Serves 6–8

INGREDIENTS

6 tbsp sesame oil
1³/₄ lb chicken meat
¹/₂ cup flour, seasoned
32 shallots, sliced
6 cups wild mushrooms, roughly
   chopped

1¹/₄ cups chicken stock
2 tbsp Worcestershire sauce
1 tbsp honey
2 tbsp grated fresh gingerroot
²/₃ cup yogurt
salt and pepper

flat leaf parsley, to garnish
wild rice and white rice, to serve

1 Heat the oil in a large skillet. Coat the chicken in the seasoned flour and cook for about 4 minutes, until browned all over. Transfer to a large deep casserole and keep warm until required.

2 Slowly fry the shallots and mushrooms in the juices.

3 Add the chicken stock, Worcestershire sauce, honey, and fresh ginger, then season.

4 Pour the mixture over the chicken, and cover the casserole with a lid or cooking foil.

5 Cook in the center of a preheated oven, 300°F, for about 1½ hours, until the meat is very tender. Add the yogurt and cook for a further 10 minutes. Serve the casserole with a mixture of wild rice and white rice and garnish with fresh parsley.

COOK'S TIP

Mushrooms can be stored in the refrigerator for 24–36 hours. Keep them in paper bags as they sweat in plastic. You do not need to peel mushrooms but wild mushrooms must be washed thoroughly.

Country Chicken Braise with Rosemary Dumplings

Root vegetables are always cheap and nutritious, and combined with chicken they make tasty and economical casseroles.

Serves 4

INGREDIENTS

4 chicken quarters
2 tbsp sunflower oil
2 medium leeks
1 cup carrots, chopped
2 cups parsnips, chopped
2 small turnips, chopped

2$^1/_2$ cups chicken stock
3 tbsp Worcestershire sauce
2 sprigs fresh rosemary
salt and pepper

DUMPLINGS:
1$^3/_4$ cups self-rising flour
3$^1/_2$ oz shredded suet
1 tbsp chopped rosemary leaves
cold water, to mix

1 Remove the skin from the chicken if you prefer. Heat the oil in a large, flameproof casserole or heavy saucepan and fry the chicken until golden. Using a draining spoon, remove the chicken from the pan. Drain off the excess fat.

2 Trim and slice the leeks. Add the carrots, parsnips, and turnips to the casserole and cook for 5 minutes, until lightly colored. Return the chicken to the pan.

3 Add the chicken stock, Worcestershire sauce, rosemary, and seasoning, then bring to the boil.

4 Reduce the heat, cover and simmer gently for about 50 minutes or until the juices run clear when the chicken is pierced with a skewer.

5 To make the dumplings, combine the flour, suet, and rosemary leaves with salt and pepper in a bowl. Stir in just enough cold water to bind to a firm dough.

6 Form into 8 small balls and place on top of the chicken and vegetables. Cover and simmer for a further 10–12 minutes, until the dumplings are well risen. Serve with the casserole.

Hungarian Chicken Goulash

*Goulash is traditionally made with beef, but this recipe successfully uses chicken instead.
To reduce fat, use a low-fat cream in place of the soured cream.*

Serves 6

INGREDIENTS

1³/4 lb chicken meat, diced
¹/2 cup flour, seasoned with 1 tsp
   paprika, salt and pepper
2 tbsp olive oil
2 tbsp butter
1 onion, sliced
24 shallots, peeled

1 each red and green
   bell pepper, chopped
1 tbsp paprika
1 tsp rosemary, crushed
4 tbsp tomato paste
1¹/4 cups chicken stock
²/3 cup claret

14 oz can chopped tomatoes
²/3 cup soured cream
1 tbsp chopped fresh parsley,
   to garnish
chunks of bread and a side salad,
   to serve

1 Toss the chicken in the seasoned flour until it is coated all over.

2 In a flameproof casserole, heat the oil and butter and fry the onion, shallots, and bell peppers for 3 minutes.

3 Add the chicken and cook for a further 4 minutes.

4 Sprinkle with the paprika and rosemary.

5 Add the tomato paste, chicken stock, claret, and chopped tomatoes, cover, and cook in the center of a preheated oven, 325°F for 1¹/2 hours.

6 Remove the casserole from the oven, allow it to stand for 4 minutes, add the soured cream, and garnish with parsley.

7 Serve with chunks of bread and a side salad.

VARIATION

Serve the goulash with buttered ribbon noodles instead of bread. For an authentic touch, try a Hungarian red wine instead of the claret.

Bourguignonne of Chicken

A recipe based on a classic French dish. Use a good quality wine when making this casserole.

Serves 4-6

INGREDIENTS

4 tbsp sunflower oil
1³/₄ lb chicken meat, diced
3 cups button mushrooms
²/₃ cup rindless,
   smoked bacon, diced
16 shallots

2 garlic cloves, crushed
1 tbsp all-purpose flour
²/₃ cup white Burgundy wine
²/₃ cup chicken stock

1 bouquet garni (1 bay leaf, sprig
   thyme, stick of celery, parsley, and
   sage tied with string)
salt and pepper
deep-fried croutons and a selection
   of cooked vegetables, to serve

1 Heat the sunflower oil in an ovenproof casserole and brown the chicken all over. Remove from the casserole with a slotted spoon.

2 Add the mushrooms, bacon, shallots, and garlic to the casserole and cook for 4 minutes.

3 Return the chicken to the casserole and sprinkle with flour. Cook for a further 2 minutes, stirring.

4 Add the Burgundy wine and chicken stock to the casserole and stir until boiling. Add the bouquet garni and season well with salt and pepper.

5 Cover the casserole and bake in the center of a preheated oven, 200°F, for 1½ hours. Remove the bouquet garni.

6 Deep fry 8 heart-shaped croutons in beef drippings and serve with the bourguignonne.

COOK'S TIP

A good quality red wine can be used instead of the white wine, to produce a rich, glossy red sauce.

Fricassée of Chicken in Lime Sauce

The addition of lime juice and lime peel adds a delicious tangy flavor to this chicken stew.

Serves 4

INGREDIENTS

1 large chicken, cut into
    small portions
½ cup flour, seasoned
2 tbsp oil
1 lb 2 oz baby onions
    or shallots, sliced

1 each green and red bell pepper,
    sliced thinly
⅔ cup chicken stock
juice and peel of 2 limes
2 chilies, chopped
2 tbsp oyster sauce

1 tsp Worcestershire sauce
salt and pepper

1 Coat the chicken pieces in the seasoned flour. Heat the oil in a large skillet and cook the chicken for about 4 minutes until browned all over.

2 Using a draining spoon, transfer the chicken to a large, deep casserole and sprinkle with the sliced onions. Keep warm until required.

3 Slowly fry the bell peppers in the juices remaining in the skillet.

4 Add the chicken stock, lime juice, and peel, and cook for a further 5 minutes.

5 Add the chilies, oyster sauce, and Worcestershire sauce. Season with salt and pepper to taste.

6 Pour the bell peppers and juices over the chicken and onions.

7 Cover the casserole with a lid or cooking foil.

8 Cook in the center of a preheated oven, 375°F, for 1½ hours until the chicken is very tender, then serve.

COOK'S TIP

Try this casserole with a cheese biscuit topping. About 30 minutes before the end of cooking time, simply top with rounds cut from cheese biscuit pastry.

Spiced Chicken Casserole

Spices, herbs, fruit, nuts, and vegetables are combined to make an appealing casserole with lots of flavor.

Serves 4–6

INGREDIENTS

3 tbsp olive oil
2 lb chicken meat, sliced
10 shallots or pickling onions
3 carrots, chopped
^{1}/2 cup chestnuts, sliced
^{1}/2 cup slivered almonds, toasted
1 tsp freshly grated nutmeg
3 tsp ground cinnamon
1^1/4 cups white wine

1^1/4 cups chicken stock
/4 cup white wine vinegar
1 tbsp chopped fresh tarragon
1 tbsp chopped fresh flat leaf parsley
1 tbsp chopped fresh thyme
grated peel of 1 orange
1 tbsp dark muscovado sugar
^{3}/4 cup seedless black grapes, halved
sea salt and pepper

fresh herbs, to garnish
wild rice or puréed potato, to serve

1 Heat the olive oil in a large saucepan and fry the chicken, shallots or pickling onions, and carrots for about 6 minutes or until browned.

2 Add the remaining ingredients, except the grapes, and simmer over a low heat for 2 hours until the meat is very tender. Stir the casserole occasionally.

3 Add the grapes just before serving and serve with wild rice or puréed potato. Garnish with herbs.

VARIATION

Experiment with different types of nuts and fruits – try sunflower seeds instead of the almonds, and add 2 fresh apricots, chopped.

COOK'S TIP

This casserole would also be delicious served with thick slices of crusty whole wheat bread to soak up the sauce.

Suprême of Chicken with Black Cherries

This recipe is rather time-consuming but it is well worth the effort.
Cherries and chicken make a good flavor combination.

Serves 6

INGREDIENTS

6 large chicken suprêmes
6 black peppercorns, crushed
2 cups pitted black cherries, or
  canned pitted cherries
12 shallots, sliced

4 slices rindless, streaky bacon,
  chopped
8 juniper berries
4 tbsp port
^{2}/3 cup red wine
2 tbsp butter

2 tbsp walnut oil
^{1}/4 cup flour
salt and pepper
new potatoes and green beans,
  to serve

1 Place the chicken in an ovenproof dish. Add the peppercorns, cherries, or canned cherries, and their juice, if using, and the shallots.

2 Add the bacon, juniper berries, port, and red wine. Season well.

3 Place the chicken in the refrigerator and leave to marinate for 48 hours.

4 Heat the butter and walnut oil in a large skillet. Remove the chicken from the marinade and fry quickly in the pan for 4 minutes on each side.

5 Return the chicken to the marinade, reserving the butter, oil, and juices in the pan.

6 Cover with foil and bake in a preheated oven, 350°F, for 20 minutes. Transfer the chicken from the baking pan to a warm serving dish. Add the flour to the juices in the skillet and cook for 4 minutes, add the marinade, and bring to the boil then simmer for 10 minutes until the sauce reaches a smooth consistency.

7 Pour the cherry sauce over the chicken suprêmes and serve with new potatoes and green beans.

Chicken with Baby Onions & Green Peas

Pork fat adds a tasty flavor to this dish. If you can't find fresh garden peas, frozen peas are a good substitute.

Serves 4

INGREDIENTS

1 cup pork fat, cut into small cubes
4 tbsp butter
16 small onions or shallots

2 lb 4 oz boneless chicken pieces
$1/4$ cup all-purpose flour
$2^1/2$ cups chicken stock

bouquet garni
4 cups fresh peas
salt and pepper

1 Bring a saucepan of salted water to the boil and simmer the pork fat cubes for three minutes. Drain and dry the pork on paper towels.

2 Melt the butter in a large skillet, add the pork and onions, and fry gently for 3 minutes until lightly browned.

3 Remove the pork and onions from the pan and set aside until required. Add the chicken pieces to the pan and cook until browned all over. Transfer the chicken to an ovenproof casserole.

4 Add the flour to the pan and cook, stirring until it begins to brown, then slowly blend in the chicken stock.

5 Cook the chicken, with the sauce and bouquet garni, in a preheated oven, 400°F, for 35 minutes.

6 Remove the bouquet garni about 10 minutes before the end of cooking time and add the peas and the reserved pork and onions. Stir to mix.

7 When cooked, place the chicken pieces on to a large platter, surrounded with the pork, peas, and onions.

COOK'S TIP

If you want to cut down on fat, use lean bacon, cut into small cubes, rather than pork fat.

Rustic Chicken & Orange Pot

*Low in fat and high in fiber, this colorful casserole
makes a healthy and hearty meal.*

Serves 4

INGREDIENTS

8 chicken drumsticks, skinned
1 tbsp whole wheat flour
1 tbsp olive oil
2 medium red onions
1 garlic clove, crushed
1 tsp fennel seeds
1 bay leaf

finely grated peel and juice
  of 1 small orange
14 oz can chopped tomatoes
14 oz can cannellini
  or flageolet beans, drained
salt and black pepper

TOPPING:
3 thick slices whole wheat bread
2 tsp olive oil

1 Toss the chicken drumsticks in the flour to coat evenly. Heat the oil in a non-stick or heavy saucepan and fry the chicken over a fairly high heat, turning frequently, until golden brown. Transfer to a large ovenproof casserole and keep warm until required.

2 Slice the red onions into thin wedges. Add to the pan and cook for a few minutes until lightly browned. Stir in the garlic.

3 Add the fennel seeds, bay leaf, orange peel and juice, tomatoes, beans, and seasoning.

4 Cover tightly and cook in a preheated oven, 375°F, for 30–35 minutes until the chicken juices are clear and not pink when pierced through the thickest part with a metal skewer.

5 For the topping, cut the bread into small dice and toss in the oil. Remove the lid from the casserole and top with the bread cubes. Bake for a further 15–20 minutes until the bread is golden and crisp. Serve hot.

COOK'S TIP

Choose beans which are canned in water, with no added sugar or salt. Drain and rinse well before use.

Californian Chicken

*It is better if you have time to bone the chicken completely,
or use chicken breast after removing all the fat and skin.*

Serves 4-6

INGREDIENTS

1 1/2 cups all-purpose flour
1 tsp paprika
1 tsp freeze-dried Italian seasoning
1 tsp freeze-dried tarragon
1 tsp rosemary, finely crushed
2 eggs, beaten
1/2 cup milk

1 chicken, weighing about
   4 lb, jointed
seasoned flour
2/3 cup rapeseed oil
2 bananas, quartered
1 apple, cut into rings,

12 oz can corn-on-the-cob &
   peppers, drained
oil for frying
salt and pepper
peppercorn or horseradish sauce,
   to serve

1 Mix together the flour, spices, herbs, and a pinch of salt in a large bowl. Make a well in the center and add the eggs.

2 Blend and slowly add the milk, whisking until very smooth.

3 Coat the chicken pieces with seasoned flour and dip the chicken pieces into the batter mix.

4 Heat the oil in a large skillet. Add the chicken and fry for

about 3 minutes or until lightly browned all over. Place the chicken pieces on a non-stick cookie sheet.

5 Batter the bananas and apple rings and fry for 2 minutes.

6 Finally toss the corn-on-the-cob into the leftover batter.

7 Heat a little oil in a skillet. Drop in spoonfuls of the corn mixture to make flat patty cakes. Cook for 4 minutes on each side.

Keep warm with the apple and banana fritters.

8 Bake the chicken in a preheated oven, 400°F, for about 25 minutes until the chicken is tender and golden brown.

9 Arrange the chicken, corn fritters, and the apple and banana fritters, on a bed of fresh watercress. Serve with a peppercorn or horseradish sauce.

Sage Chicken & Rice

Cooking in a single pot means that all of the flavors are retained.
This is a substantial meal that needs only a salad and some crusty bread.

Serves 4

INGREDIENTS

1 large onion, chopped
1 garlic clove, minced
2 sticks celery, sliced
2 carrots, diced
2 sprigs fresh sage
1¼ cups chicken stock
12 oz boneless, skinless chicken
   breasts

1⅓ cups mixed brown and wild rice
14 oz can chopped tomatoes
dash of Tabasco sauce
2 medium zucchini, trimmed and
   thinly sliced
3½ oz lean ham, diced
salt and pepper
fresh sage, to garnish

TO SERVE:
salad leaves
crusty bread

1 Place the onion, garlic, celery, carrots, and sprigs of fresh sage in a large saucepan and pour in the chicken stock. Bring to the boil, cover the pan, and simmer for 5 minutes.

2 Cut the chicken into 1 inch cubes and stir into the pan with the vegetables. Cover the pan and continue to cook for a further 5 minutes.

3 Stir in the rice and chopped tomatoes. Add a dash of Tabasco sauce to taste and season well. Bring to the boil, cover, and simmer for 25 minutes.

4 Stir in the sliced zucchini and diced ham and continue to cook, uncovered, for a further 10 minutes, stirring occasionally, until the rice is just tender.

5 Remove and discard the sprigs of sage. Garnish with a few sage leaves and serve with a fresh salad and crusty bread.

COOK'S TIP

If you do not have fresh sage,
use 1 tsp of dried sage in step 1.

Chicken & Plum Casserole

Full of the flavors of fall, this combination of lean chicken, shallots, garlic, and fresh, juicy plums is a very fruity blend. Serve with bread to mop up the gravy.

Serves 4

INGREDIENTS

2 rashers lean back bacon, rinds
   removed, trimmed and chopped
1 tbsp sunflower oil
1 lb skinless, boneless chicken thighs,
   cut into 4 equal strips
1 garlic clove, crushed
6 oz shallots, halved

8 oz plums, halved or quartered (if
   large) and stoned
1 tbsp light muscovado sugar
$^2/_3$ cup dry sherry
2 tbsp plum sauce
2 cups fresh chicken stock

2 tsp cornstarch mixed with 4 tsp
   cold water
2 tbsp fresh parsley, chopped,
   to garnish
crusty bread, to serve

1 In a large, non-stick skillet, dry fry the bacon for 2–3 minutes until the juices run out. Remove the bacon from the pan with a draining spoon, set aside, and keep warm.

2 In the same skillet, heat the oil and fry the chicken with the garlic and shallots for 4–5 minutes, stirring occasionally, until well browned all over.

3 Return the bacon to the pan and stir in the plums, sugar, sherry, plum sauce, and stock. Bring to the boil and simmer for 20 minutes until the plums have softened and the chicken is cooked through.

4 Add the cornstarch mixture to the pan and cook, stirring, for a further 2–3 minutes until thickened.

5 Spoon the casserole on to warm serving plates and garnish with chopped parsley. Serve with chunks of bread to mop up the fruity gravy.

VARIATION

Chunks of lean turkey or pork would also go well with this combination of flavors. The cooking time will remain the same.

Chicken Marengo

Napoleon's chef was ordered to cook a sumptuous meal on the eve of the battle of Marengo.
He gathered everything possible to make a feast, and this was the result.

Serves 4

INGREDIENTS

1 tbsp olive oil
8 chicken pieces
10^1/$_2$ oz tomato paste
^{3}/$_4$ cup white wine
2 tsp dried mixed herbs
8 slices white bread

1^1/$_2$ oz butter, melted
2 garlic cloves, crushed
3^1/$_2$ oz mixed mushrooms (such as
   button, oyster, and ceps)

1^3/$_4$ oz black olives, chopped
1 tsp sugar
fresh basil, to garnish

1 Using a sharp knife, remove the bone from each of the chicken pieces.

2 Heat the oil in a large skillet. Add the chicken pieces and cook for 4–5 minutes, turning occasionally, or until browned all over.

3 Add the tomato paste, wine, and mixed herbs to the skillet. Bring to the boil and then leave to simmer for 30 minutes or until the chicken is tender and the juices run clear when a skewer is inserted into the thickest part of the meat.

4 Mix the melted butter and crushed garlic together. Lightly toast the slices of bread and brush with the garlic butter.

5 Add the remaining oil to a separate skillet and cook the mushrooms for 2–3 minutes or until just brown.

6 Add the olives and sugar to the chicken mixture and warm through.

COOK'S TIP

If you have time, marinate the chicken pieces in the wine and herbs and leave in the refrigerator for 2 hours. This will make the chicken more tender and accentuate the wine flavor of the sauce.

Barbecues & Broils

There is nothing more delicious than the juicy flesh and charred skin of chicken that has been grilled over an open fire – after marinating in a flavorful mixture of oil and herbs or spices. Try an Asian-style mixture of yogurt and aromatic spices, or soy sauce, sesame oil, and fresh gingerroot. There are some unusual flavors and innovative tastes, including Skewered Chicken with Bramble Sauce, and Skewered Chicken Spirals, which are attractive whirls of chicken, bacon, and basil. Baby chickens, flavored with lemon and tarragon in this section, are perfect for broiling or barbecuing. There is also a recipe for Broiled Chicken Salad which combines chicken breasts with a selection of broiled vegetables including zucchini, eggplant, and bell pepper drizzled with olive oil and served with crusty bread to soak up the delicious juices.

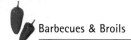
Favorite Grilled Chicken

These chicken wings are brushed with a simple grill glaze, which can be made in minutes, but the results are sure to delight everyone.

Serves 4

INGREDIENTS

8 chicken wings or 1 chicken cut into
  8 portions
3 tbsp tomato paste

3 tbsp brown fruity sauce
1 tbsp white wine vinegar
1 tbsp honey

1 tbsp olive oil
1 clove garlic, crushed (optional)
salad greens, to serve

1 Remove the skin from the chicken if you want to reduce the fat in the dish.

2 To make the barbecue glaze, place the tomato paste, brown fruity sauce, white wine vinegar, honey, oil, and garlic in a small bowl. Stir all of the ingredients together until they are thoroughly blended.

3 Brush the grill glaze over the chicken and grill over hot coals for 15–20 minutes. Turn the chicken portions over occasionally and baste frequently with the grill glaze. If the chicken begins to blacken before it is cooked, raise the rack if possible or move the chicken to a cooler part of the grill to slow down the cooking.

4 Transfer the grilled chicken to warm serving plates and serve with fresh salad leaves.

VARIATION

This grill glaze also makes a very good baste to brush over pork chops.

COOK'S TIP

When poultry is cooked over a very hot grill, the heat immediately seals in all of the juices, leaving the meat succulent. For this reason make sure that the coals are hot enough before starting to grill.

Broiled Chicken & Vegetable Salad

Broiling is a quick, healthy cooking method, ideal for sealing in the juices and flavor of chicken breasts, and a wonderful way to cook summer vegetables.

Serves 4

INGREDIENTS

1 small eggplant, sliced
2 garlic cloves, crushed
finely grated rind of $^1/_2$ lemon
1 tbsp chopped fresh mint
6 tbsp olive oil
4 boneless chicken breasts

2 medium zucchini, sliced
1 medium red bell pepper, quartered
1 small bulb fennel, sliced thickly
1 large red onion, sliced thickly

1 small ciabatta loaf or
 1 French baguette, sliced
extra olive oil
salt and pepper

1 Place the eggplant slices in a colander and sprinkle with salt. Leave over a bowl to drain for 30 minutes, rinse, and dry. This will get rid of the bitter juices.

2 Mix together the garlic, lemon peel, mint, and olive oil, and season.

3 Slash the chicken breasts at intervals with a sharp knife. Spoon over about half of the oil

mixture and stir to combine all the ingredients.

4 Combine the eggplants and the remaining vegetables, then toss in the remaining oil mixture. Marinate the chicken and vegetables for about 30 minutes.

5 Place the chicken breasts and vegetables on a preheated hot broiler or grill, and turning occasionally, until they are golden

brown and tender, or cook on a ridged griddle pan on the hob.

6 Brush the bread slices with olive oil and broil until golden.

7 Drizzle a little olive oil over the chicken and grilled vegetables and serve hot or cold with the crusty bread toasts.

Chicken with Garden Herbs

Warm weather calls for lighter eating, and this chilled chicken dish in a subtle herb vinaigrette is ideal for a summer dinner party, or for a picnic.

Serves 4

INGREDIENTS

4 part-boned, skinless
  chicken breasts
6 tbsp olive oil
2 tbsp lemon juice

4 tbsp finely chopped summer herbs,
  such as parsley, chives and mint
1 ripe avocado

$1/2$ cup low-fat fromage blanc
pepper
cold rice, to serve

1 Using a sharp knife, cut 3–4 deep slashes in the chicken breasts.

2 Place in a flameproof dish and brush lightly with a little of the olive oil.

3 Cook the chicken on a preheated moderately hot broiler turning once until golden and the juices run clear when the chicken is pierced in the thickest part with a skewer.

4 Combine the remaining oil with the lemon juice and herbs and season with pepper. Spoon the oil over the chicken and leave to cool. Chill in the refrigerator for at least 1 hour.

5 Mash the avocado or purée in a food processor with the fromage blanc. Season with pepper to taste. Serve the chicken with the avocado sauce and rice.

COOK'S TIP

The chicken can be cooked several hours before you need it and stored in the refrigerator until required.

COOK'S TIP

To remove the stone easily from an avocado, first cut the avocado in half. Holding one half securely in your hand, rap the knife into the stone so that it becomes embedded in the stone, then carefully twist the knife to dislodge the stone.

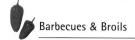

Spatchcock Baby Chicken with Garlic & Herbs

*It is not difficult to spatchcock open out baby chickens,
and it is the best way to cook whole birds on the grill.*

Serves 2

INGREDIENTS

2 baby chickens, each 1lb
³/₄ oz butter
2 cloves garlic, crushed
2 tbsp chopped, mixed fresh herbs

BASTE:
4 tbsp olive oil
2 tbsp lemon juice

2 tbsp chopped, mixed herbs
salt and pepper

1 To spatchcock each chicken, place each bird on its breast and use sharp scissors or poultry shears to cut along the length of the back bone. Open out the bird as much as possible and place it breast-side up on a chopping board. Press down firmly on the breast bone to break it.

2 Mix together the butter, garlic and herbs until well combined. Lift up the skin from the breast of each chicken. Divide the butter equally between the 2 chickens and spread over the breast under the skin.

3 Open out each bird. Thread 2 skewers diagonally through each bird to hold it flat.

4 Mix together the ingredients for the baste in a bowl.

5 Place the birds, bone-side down, over medium hot coals and grill for 25 minutes, basting with the lemon and herb baste. Turn the birds over and grill, skin-side down, for 15 minutes, basting frequently, or until cooked through.

COOK'S TIP

Use a combination of whatever fresh herbs you have to hand. Thyme, rosemary, mint, oregano, parsley, or cilantro are all suitable. If you want to cook a whole chicken in this way double the amount of baste and cook for 40–50 minutes.

Broiled Poussin with Lemon & Tarragon

Spatchcocked baby chickens are complemented by the delicate fragrance of lemon and tarragon and broiled.

Serves 2

INGREDIENTS

2 baby chickens
4 sprigs fresh tarragon
1 tsp oil
2 tbsp butter

peel of $\frac{1}{2}$ lemon
1 tbsp lemon juice
1 garlic clove, crushed
salt and pepper

tarragon and orange slices,
  to garnish

1 Prepare the baby chickens, turn them breast-side down on a chopping board and cut them through the backbone using kitchen scissors. Crush each bird gently to break the bones so that they lie flat while cooking. Season each with salt.

2 Turn them over and insert a sprig of tarragon under the skin over each side of the breast.

3 Brush the chickens with oil, using a pastry brush, and place under a preheated hot broiler about 5 inches from the heat. Broil the chickens for about 15 minutes, turning half way, until they are lightly browned.

4 Meanwhile, to make the glaze, melt the butter in a small saucepan, add the lemon peel, lemon juice, and garlic, and season with salt and pepper.

5 Brush the baby chickens with the glaze and cook for a further 15 minutes, turning them once and brushing regularly so that they stay moist. Garnish the chickens with tarragon and orange slices and serve with new potatoes.

COOK'S TIP

Once the chickens are flattened, insert 2 metal skewers through them to keep them flat.

Broiled Chicken Quarters with Warm Aioli

Chicken quarters are grilled, then served with a strongly flavored garlic mayonnaise, which originated in Provence, France.

Serves 4

INGREDIENTS

4 chicken quarters
2 tbsp oil
2 tbsp lemon juice
2 tsp dried thyme
salt and pepper

green salad and lemon slices, to serve

AIOLI:
5 garlic cloves, minced
2 egg yolks

$^1/_2$ cup each olive oil and sunflower oil
2 tsp lemon juice
2 tbsp boiling water

1 Using a skewer, prick the chicken quarters in several places and place them in a shallow dish.

2 Combine the oil, lemon juice, thyme, and seasoning, then pour over the chicken, turning to coat the chicken evenly. Set aside for 2 hours.

3 To make the aioli, beat together the garlic and a pinch of salt to make a paste. Add the egg yolks and beat well.

Gradually add the oils, drop by drop, beating vigorously, until the mayonnaise becomes creamy and smooth. Add the oils in a thin steady trickle and continue beating until the aioli is thick. Stir in the lemon juice and season with pepper. Set aside in a warm place.

4 Place the chicken on a preheated grill and cook for 25–30 minutes. Brush with the marinade and turn the portions to cook evenly. Remove and arrange on a serving plate.

5 Beat the water into the aioli and turn into a warmed serving bowl. Serve the chicken with the aioli, a green salad, and lemon slices.

COOK'S TIP

To make a quick aioli, add the garlic to $1^1/_4$ cups good quality mayonnaise then place in a bowl over a pan of warm water and beat together. Just before serving add 1–2 tbsp hot water.

Broiled Chicken with Pesto Toasts

This Italian-style dish is richly flavored with pesto, which is a mixture of basil, olive oil, pine nuts, and Parmesan cheese. Either red or green pesto can be used for this recipe.

Serves 4

INGREDIENTS

8 part-boned chicken thighs
olive oil, for brushing
1²/₃ cups sieved tomatoes

/2 cup green
   or red pesto sauce
12 slices French bread
1 cup freshly grated
   Parmesan cheese

¹/₂ cup pine nuts
   or slivered almonds
salad leaves, to serve

1 Arrange the chicken in a single layer in a wide flameproof dish and brush lightly with oil. Place under a preheated broiler for about 15 minutes, turning occasionally, until golden brown.

2 Pierce the chicken with a skewer to ensure that there is no trace of pink in the juices.

3 Pour off any excess fat. Warm the sieved tomatoes and half the pesto sauce in a small pan and pour over the chicken. Broil for a few more minutes, turning until coated.

4 Meanwhile, spread the remaining pesto on to the slices of bread. Arrange the bread over the chicken and sprinkle with the Parmesan cheese. Scatter the pine nuts over the cheese. Broil for 2–3 minutes, or until browned and bubbling. Serve with a selection of salad leaves.

COOK'S TIP

Although leaving the skin on the chicken means that it will have a higher fat content, many people like the rich taste and crispy skin especially when it is blackened by the grill. The skin also keeps in the cooking juices.

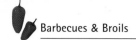
Sweet Maple Chicken

You can use any chicken portions for this recipe. Boned chicken thighs are economical for large barbecue parties, but you could also use wings or drumsticks.

Serves 6

INGREDIENTS

2 boned chicken thighs
5 tbsp maple syrup
1 tbsp superfine sugar
grated peel and juice of $\frac{1}{2}$ orange
2 tbsp tomato catsup

2 tsp Worcestershire sauce

TO GARNISH:
slices of orange
sprig of flat-leaf parsley

TO SERVE:
focaccia bread
salad leaves
cherry tomatoes, quartered

1 Using a sharp knife, make 2–3 slashes in the flesh of the chicken. Place the chicken in a shallow, nonmetallic dish.

2 To make the marinade, mix together the maple syrup, sugar, orange peel, and juice, catsup, and Worcestershire sauce in a small bowl.

3 Pour the marinade over the chicken, tossing the chicken to coat thoroughly. Cover and leave to chill in the refrigerator until required.

4 Remove the chicken from the marinade, reserving the marinade for basting.

5 Transfer the chicken to the grill and cook over hot coals for 20 minutes, turning the chicken and basting with the marinade frequently.

6 Transfer the chicken to serving plates and garnish with slices of orange and a sprig of fresh-leaf parsley. Serve with focaccia bread, fresh salad greens, and cherry tomatoes.

COOK'S TIP

If time is short you can omit the marinating time. If you use chicken quarters, rather than the smaller thigh portions, par-boil them for 10 minutes before brushing with the marinade and grilling.

Minty Lime Chicken

These tangy lime and honey-coated pieces have a matching sauce or dip based on creamy unsweetened yogurt. They could be served at a barbecue or as a main course for a dinner party.

Serves 6

INGREDIENTS

3 tbsp finely chopped mint
4 tbsp clear honey
4 tbsp lime juice
12 boneless chicken thighs

SAUCE:
/2 cup unsweetened thick yogurt
1 tbsp finely chopped mint
2 tsp finely grated lime peel

1 Combine the mint, honey, and lime juice in a bowl.

2 Use toothpicks to keep the chicken thighs in neat shapes and add the chicken to the marinade, turning to coat evenly.

3 Leave to marinate for at least 30 minutes, preferably overnight. Cook the chicken on a preheated moderately hot barbecue or broiler, turning frequently and basting with the marinade. The chicken is cooked if the juices run clear when the chicken is pierced in the thickest part with a skewer.

4 Meanwhile, mix together the sauce ingredients.

5 Remove the toothpicks and serve the chicken with a salad and the sauce.

VARIATION

Use this marinade for chicken kabobs, alternating the chicken with lime and red onion wedges.

COOK'S TIP

Mint can be grown very easily in a garden or window box. It is a useful herb for marinades and salad dressings. Other useful herbs to grow are parsley and basil.

Jerk Chicken

This is perhaps one of the best known Caribbean dishes. The "jerk" in the name refers to the hot spicy coating.

Serves 4

INGREDIENTS

4 chicken portions
1 bunch scallions, trimmed
1–2 Scotch Bonnet chilies, seeded
1 garlic clove

2 inch piece gingerroot, peeled and roughly chopped
$1/2$ tsp dried thyme
$1/2$ tsp paprika
$1/4$ tsp ground allspice

pinch ground cinnamon
pinch ground cloves
4 tbsp white wine vinegar
3 tbsp light soy sauce
pepper

1 Rinse the chicken portions and pat them dry on paper towels. Place them in a shallow dish.

2 Place the scallions, chilies, garlic, ginger, thyme, paprika, allspice, cinnamon, cloves, wine vinegar, soy sauce, and pepper to taste in a food processor and process to make a smooth mixture.

3 Pour the spicy mixture over the chicken. Turn the chicken portions over so that they are well coated in the marinade. Transfer the chicken to the refrigerator and leave to marinate for up to 24 hours.

4 Remove the chicken from the marinade and grill over medium hot coals for about 30 minutes, turning the chicken over and basting occasionally with any remaining marinade, until the chicken is cooked through.

5 Transfer the chicken portions to individual serving plates and serve at once.

COOK'S TIP

As Jamaican cuisine becomes increasingly popular, you will find jars of ready-made jerk marinade, which you can use when time is short. Allow the chicken to marinate for as long as possible for maximum flavor.

VARIATION

You can use milder chilies or even increase the amount of chili used.

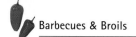

Chicken Cajun-Style

These spicy chicken wings are good served with a chili salsa and salad. Alternatively, if this is too spicy for your taste, try a sour cream and chive dip.

Serves 4

INGREDIENTS

16 chicken wings
4 tsp paprika
2 tsp ground coriander
1 tsp celery salt
1 tsp ground cumin
$^1/_2$ tsp cayenne pepper

$^1/_2$ tsp salt
1 tbsp oil
2 tbsp red wine vinegar
fresh parsley, to garnish
cherry tomatoes and mixed salad
   greens, to serve

1 Wash the chicken wings and pat dry with paper towels. Remove the wing tips with kitchen scissors.

2 Mix together the paprika, coriander, celery salt, cumin, cayenne pepper, salt, oil, and red wine vinegar.

3 Rub this mixture over the wings to coat evenly and set aside, in the refrigerator, for at least 1 hour to allow the flavors to permeate the chicken.

4 Cook the chicken wings on a preheated grill, occasionally brushing with oil, for about 15 minutes, turning often until cooked through. Garnish with fresh parsley and serve with cherry tomatoes, mixed salad greens, and a sauce of your choice.

COOK'S TIP

To save time, you can buy ready-made Cajun spice seasoning to rub over the chicken wings.

VARIATION

Although chicken wings do not have much meat on them, they are small and easy to pick up with your fingers which makes them ideal for barbecues. However, they can also be enjoyed fried or roasted.

Spicy Sesame Chicken

This is a quick and easy recipe for the grill, perfect
for lunch or to eat outdoors on a picnic.

Serves 4

INGREDIENTS

4 chicken quarters
1/2 cup unsweetened yogurt

finely grated peel and juice
   of 1 small lemon
2 tsp medium-hot curry paste

1 tbsp sesame seeds
lemon wedges, to serve

1 Remove the skin from the chicken and make cuts in the flesh at intervals with a sharp knife.

2 In a bowl, combine the unsweetened yogurt, lemon peel, lemon juice, and curry paste to form a smooth mixture.

3 Spoon the mixture over the chicken and arrange on a foil-lined broiler pan or cookie sheet.

4 Place the chicken quarters under a preheated moderately hot broiler and broil for 12–15 minutes, turning once. Broil until golden brown and thoroughly cooked. Just before the end of the cooking time, sprinkle the chicken with the sesame seeds.

5 Serve with a salad, naan bread, and lemon wedges.

COOK'S TIP

If you have time, leave the chicken and the sauce in the refrigerator to marinate overnight so the flavors are fully absorbed.

VARIATION

Poppy seeds, fennel seeds, or cumin seeds, or a mixture of all three, can also be used to sprinkle over the chicken.

Indian Charred Chicken

An Indian-influenced dish that is delicious served
with naan bread and a cucumber raita.

Serves 4

INGREDIENTS

4 chicken breasts, skinned and boned
2 tbsp curry paste
1 tbsp sunflower oil
1 tbsp light muscovado sugar
1 tsp ground ginger
$^1/_2$ tsp ground cumin

TO SERVE:
naan bread
green salad leaves

CUCUMBER RAITA:
$^1/_4$ cucumber
salt
$^2/_3$ cup unsweetened yogurt
$^1/_4$ tsp chili powder

---

1 Place the chicken breasts between 2 sheets of baking parchment or plastic wrap. Pound them with the flat side of a meat mallet or rolling pin to flatten them.

2 Mix together the curry paste, oil, sugar, ginger, and cumin in a small bowl. Spread the mixture over both sides of the chicken and set aside until required.

3 To make the raita, peel the cucumber and scoop out the seeds with a spoon. Grate the cucumber flesh, sprinkle with salt, place in a strainer, and leave to stand for 10 minutes. Rinse off the salt and squeeze out any moisture by pressing the cucumber with the base of a glass or back of a spoon.

4 To make the raita, mix the cucumber with the yogurt and stir in the chili powder. Leave to chill until required.

5 Transfer the chicken to a rack and grill for 10 minutes.

6 Warm the naan bread at the side of the barbecue. Serve the chicken with the naan bread and raita and accompanied with fresh green salad leaves.

COOK'S TIP

Flattening the chicken breasts
makes them thinner so that they
cook more quickly.

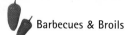

Sticky Chicken Drumsticks

These drumsticks are always popular with children - make sure there are plenty of
napkins for wiping sticky fingers or provide finger bowls with a slice of lemon.

Serves 10

INGREDIENTS

10 chicken drumsticks	1 tbsp Worcestershire sauce	TO SERVE:
4 tbsp fine-cut orange marmalade	grated peel and juice of $1/2$ orange	cherry tomatoes
	salt and pepper	salad leaves

1 Using a sharp knife, make 2–3 slashes in the flesh of each chicken drumstick.

2 Bring a large saucepan of water to a boil and add the chicken drumsticks. Cover the pan, return to a boil, and cook for 5–10 minutes. Remove the chicken and drain thoroughly.

3 Meanwhile, make the baste. Place the orange marmalade, Worcestershire sauce, orange peel and juice, and salt and pepper to taste in a small saucepan. Heat gently, stirring continuously, until the marmalade melts and all of the ingredients are well combined.

4 Brush the baste over the par-cooked chicken drumsticks and transfer them to the grill to complete cooking. Barbecue over hot coals for about 10 minutes, turning and basting frequently with the remaining baste.

5 Carefully thread 3 cherry tomatoes on to a skewer and transfer to the barbecue for 1–2 minutes.

6 Transfer the chicken drumsticks to serving plates. Serve with the cherry tomato skewers and a selection of fresh salad leaves.

COOK'S TIP

Par-cooking the chicken is an ideal way of making sure that it is cooked through without becoming overcooked and burned on the outside.

Sweet & Sour Drumsticks

Chicken drumsticks are marinated to impart a tangy sweet and sour flavor and a shiny glaze.

Serves 4

INGREDIENTS

8 chicken drumsticks
4 tbsp red wine vinegar
2 tbsp tomato paste
2 tbsp soy sauce

2 tbsp honey
1 tbsp Worcestershire sauce
1 garlic clove
good pinch cayenne pepper

salt and pepper
sprig of fresh parsley, to garnish

1 Skin the chicken, if desired, and slash 2–3 times with a sharp knife.

2 Lay the chicken drumsticks side by side in a shallow nonmetallic container.

3 Mix the red wine vinegar, tomato paste, soy sauce, honey, Worcestershire sauce, garlic, and cayenne pepper together and pour over the chicken drumsticks.

4 Leave to marinate in the refrigerator for 1 hour. Cook the drumsticks on a preheated grill for about 20 minutes, brushing with the marinade and turning during cooking. Garnish with parsley and serve with a crisp salad.

COOK'S TIP

For a tangy flavor, add the juice of 1 lime to the marinade. While the drumsticks are grilling, check regularly to ensure that they are not burning.

VARIATION

This sweet and sour marinade would also work well with pork or shrimp. Thread pork cubes or shrimp onto skewers with bell peppers and button onions.

Mustardy Barbecue Drummers

Great for grills, or for simple summer lunches and picnics,
this is an easy and tasty recipe for chicken drumsticks.

Serves 4

INGREDIENTS

10 slices smoked streaky bacon
1 garlic clove, peeled
   and minced
3 tbsp wholegrain mustard

4 tbsp fresh brown bread crumbs
8 chicken drumsticks

1 tbsp sunflower oil
fresh parsley sprigs, to garnish

1 Chop two of the bacon slices into small pieces and fry without fat for 3–4 minutes, stirring so that the bacon does not stick to the bottom of the pan. Remove from the heat and stir in the minced garlic, 2 tablespoons of wholegrain mustard, and the bread crumbs.

2 Carefully loosen the skin from each drumstick with your fingers, being careful not to tear the skin. Spoon a little of the mustard stuffing under each flap of skin, smoothing the skins over firmly afterward.

3 Wrap a bacon rasher around each drumstick, and secure with toothpicks.

4 Mix together the remaining mustard and the oil, brush over the chicken drumsticks, and cook on a preheated moderately hot barbecue or broiler for about 25 minutes, until there is no trace of pink in the juices when the thickest part of the chicken is pierced with a skewer.

5 Garnish with the parsley sprigs. The drumsticks may be served hot or cold.

COOK'S TIP

Don't cook the chicken over the hottest part of the barbecue or the outside may be charred before the center is cooked.

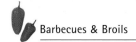

Skewered Chicken Spirals

These unusual chicken kabobs have a wonderful Mediterranean flavor, and the bacon helps keep them moist during cooking.

Serves 4

INGREDIENTS

4 skinless, boneless chicken breasts
1 garlic clove, minced
2 tbsp tomato paste

4 slices smoked back bacon
large handful fresh basil leaves
oil for brushing

salt and pepper

1 Spread out a piece of chicken between two sheets of plastic wrap and beat firmly with a rolling pin to flatten the chicken to an even thickness. Repeat with the remaining pieces of chicken.

2 Mix together the minced garlic and tomato paste until well blended. Spread the mixture evenly over the surface of the chicken.

3 Lay a bacon slice over each piece of chicken, then scatter with the fresh basil leaves. Season well with salt and pepper.

4 Roll up each piece of chicken firmly, then cut into thick slices using a sharp knife.

5 Thread the slices securely on to four skewers, making sure the skewer holds the chicken in a spiral shape.

6 Brush the skewers lightly with oil and cook on a preheated hot barbecue or grill broiler for about 5 minutes, turn the skewers over, and cook for a further 5 minutes, until the chicken is cooked through. Serve the chicken spirals hot with a green salad.

COOK'S TIP

Flattening the chicken breasts makes them thinner so that they cook more quickly. It also makes them easier to roll.

VARIATION

To complete the Mediterranean theme, serve these kabobs with Parmesan-topped garlic bread.

Chicken Skewers with Red Bell Pepper Sauce

These kabobs are rather special and are well worth the extra effort needed to prepare them.

Serves 4

INGREDIENTS

3 chicken breasts, skinned and boned
6 tbsp olive oil
4 tbsp lemon juice
$1/2$ small onion, grated
1 tbsp fresh, chopped sage
8 tbsp sage and onion stuffing mix

6 tbsp boiling water
2 green bell peppers, seeded

SAUCE:
1 tbsp olive oil

1 red bell pepper, seeded and
  chopped finely
1 small onion, chopped finely
pinch sugar
$7^1/2$ oz can chopped tomatoes

1 Cut the chicken into evenly sized pieces.

2 Mix the oil, lemon juice, grated onion, and sage, and pour the mixture into a plastic bag. Add the chicken, seal the bag, and shake to coat the chicken. Leave to marinate for at least 30 minutes, shaking the bag occasionally.

3 Place the stuffing mix in a bowl and add a boiling water, stirring to mix well.

4 Cut each bell pepper into 6 strips, then blanch them in boiling water for 3–4 minutes until softened. Drain, refresh under running water, and drain again.

5 Form about 1 teaspoon of the stuffing mixture into a ball and roll it up in a strip of bell pepper. Repeat for the remaining stuffing mixture and bell pepper strips. Thread 3 bell pepper rolls on to each skewer alternately with pieces of chicken. Leave to chill.

6 To make the sauce, heat the oil in a small pan and fry the red bell pepper and onion for 5 minutes. Add the sugar and tomatoes and simmer for about 5 minutes. Set aside and keep warm.

7 Grill the skewers on an oiled rack over hot coals, basting frequently with the remaining marinade, for about 15 minutes until the chicken is cooked. Serve with the red bell pepper sauce.

Skewered Spicy Tomato Chicken

These low-fat, spicy skewers are cooked in a matter of minutes – and they can be assembled ahead of time and stored in the refrigerator until you need them.

Serves 4

INGREDIENTS

1 lb 2 oz skinless, boneless
  chicken breasts
3 tbsp tomato paste

2 tbsp honey
2 tbsp Worcestershire sauce
1 tbsp chopped fresh rosemary

9 oz cherry tomatoes
sprigs of rosemary, to garnish
couscous or rice, to serve

1 Using a sharp knife, cut the chicken into 1 inch chunks and place in a bowl.

2 Mix together the tomato paste, honey, Worcestershire sauce, and rosemary. Add to the chicken, stirring to coat evenly.

3 Alternating the chicken pieces and tomatoes, thread them on to eight wooden skewers.

4 Spoon over any remaining glaze. Cook under a preheated hot broiler for 8–10 minutes, turning occasionally, until the chicken is thoroughly cooked. Serve on a bed of couscous or rice and garnish with sprigs of rosemary.

COOK'S TIP

Couscous is made from semolina that has been made into separate grains. It is very easy to prepare – simply soak it in a bowl of boiling water and then fluff up the grains with a fork. Flavorings such as lemon or nutmeg can be added.

COOK'S TIP

Cherry tomatoes are ideal for barbecues as they can be threaded straight on to skewers. As they are kept whole, the skins keep in the tomatoes' natural juices.

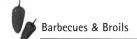

Chicken Skewers with Lemon & Cilantro

A tangy lemon yogurt is served with this tasty chicken dish.

Serves 4

INGREDIENTS

4 chicken breasts, skinned and boned
1 tsp ground coriander
2 tsp lemon juice

1¼ cups unsweetened yogurt
1 lemon

2 tbsp chopped, fresh cilantro
oil for brushing
salt and pepper

1 Cut the chicken into 1 inch pieces and place them in a shallow, nonmetallic dish.

2 Add the coriander, lemon juice, salt and pepper to taste, and 4 tbsp of the yogurt to the chicken and mix together until thoroughly combined. Cover and leave to chill for at least 2 hours, preferably overnight.

3 To make the lemon yogurt, peel and finely chop the lemon, discarding any pips. Stir the lemon into the yogurt together with the fresh cilantro. Leave to chill in the refrigerator until required.

4 Thread the chicken pieces on to skewers. Brush the rack with oil and grill the chicken over hot coals for about 15 minutes, basting with the oil.

5 Transfer the chicken kabobs to warm serving plates and garnish with a sprig of fresh cilantro, lemon wedges, and fresh salad leaves. Serve with the lemon yogurt.

COOK'S TIP

These kabobs are delicious served on a bed of blanched spinach, which has been seasoned with salt, pepper, and nutmeg.

VARIATION

Prepare the chicken the day before it is needed so that it can marinate overnight. This will allow the flavors to be fully absorbed.

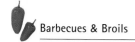
Ginger Chicken & Corn

Chicken wings and corn in a sticky ginger marinade are designed to be eaten with the fingers – there's no other way!

Serves 6

INGREDIENTS

3 cobs fresh corn-on-the-cob
12 chicken wings
1 inch piece fresh gingerroot

6 tbsp lemon juice
4 tsp sunflower oil
1 tbsp superfine sugar

1 Remove the husks and silken hairs from the corn. Using a sharp knife, cut each cob into 6 slices. Place in a large bowl with the chicken wings.

2 Peel and grate the gingerroot or chop finely.

3 Mix the ginger root with the lemon juice, sunflower oil, and superfine sugar, then toss with the corn and chicken to coat.

4 Thread the corn and chicken wings onto skewers, to make turning easier.

5 Cook the corn and chicken under a preheated moderately hot broiler or grill for 15–20 minutes, basting with the gingery glaze and turning frequently until the corn is golden brown and tender, and the chicken is cooked. Serve with jacket potatoes or salad.

COOK'S TIP

Cut off the wing tips before broiling as they burn very easily. Alternatively, you can cover them with small pieces of foil.

COOK'S TIP

When you are buying fresh corn, look for plump, tightly packed kernels. If fresh corn is unavailable, you can use thawed frozen corn instead.

Chicken Kabobs

These kabobs are a deliciously different way of serving chicken.
Serve with dhal and chapatis.

Serves 6–8

INGREDIENTS

3 lb 5 oz chicken, boned
1/2 tsp ground cumin
4 cardamom seeds, minced
1/2 tsp ground cinnamon
1 tsp salt
1 tsp fresh gingerroot, finely
    chopped

1 tsp fresh garlic, minced
1/2 tsp ground allspice
1/2 tsp pepper
1 1/4 cups water
2 tbsp yogurt
2 green chilies

1 small onion
fresh cilantro leaves
1 medium egg, beaten
1 1/4 cups oil
salad greens and lemon wedges, to
    garnish

1 Place the boned chicken in a large saucepan. Add the ground cumin, cardamom seeds, ground cinnamon, salt, ginger, garlic, ground allspice, and pepper and pour in the water. Bring the mixture to a boil until all of the water has been absorbed.

2 Put the mixture in a food processor and grind to form a smooth paste. Transfer the paste to a mixing bowl. Add the yogurt and blend together until well combined.

3 Place the green chilies, onion, and cilantro leaves in the food processor and grind finely. Add to the chicken mixture and mix well. Add the beaten egg and mix to combine.

4 Break off 12–15 portions from the mixture and make small, flat round shapes in the palm of your hand.

5 Heat the oil in a saucepan and fry the kabobs gently, in batches, over a low heat, turning once. Drain thoroughly on kitchen paper and serve hot.

COOK'S TIP

Indian kabob dishes are not necessarily cooked on a skewer; they can also be served in a dish and are always dry dishes with no sauce.

Maryland Chicken Kabobs

*A barbecue variation of the traditional dish,
Chicken Maryland. Serve with corn-on-the-cob.*

Serves 4

INGREDIENTS

8 chicken thighs, skinned and boned
1 tbsp white wine vinegar
1 tbsp lemon juice
1 tbsp golden syrup or honey
6 tbsp olive oil

1 clove garlic, minced
4 rashers rindless, smoked, streaky
  bacon
2 bananas
salt and pepper

TO SERVE:
4 cooked corn
mango relish

1 Cut the chicken into bite-size pieces. Combine the vinegar, lemon juice, syrup or honey, oil, garlic, and salt and pepper to taste in a large bowl. Add the chicken to the marinade and toss until the chicken is well coated. Cover and leave to marinate for 1-2 hours.

2 Stretch the bacon rashers with the back of a knife and then cut each bacon rasher in half. Cut the bananas into 1 inch lengths and brush them with lemon juice to prevent any discoloration.

3 Wrap a piece of bacon around each piece of banana.

4 Remove the chicken from the marinade, reserving the marinade for basting. Thread the chicken pieces and the bacon and banana rolls alternately on to skewers.

5 Barbecue the kabobs over hot coals for 8–10 minutes until the chicken is completely cooked. Baste the kabobs with the marinade and turn the skewers frequently.

6 Serve with corn-on-the-cob and mango relish.

VARIATION

For a quick Maryland-style dish, omit the marinating time and cook the chicken thighs over hot coals for about 20 minutes, basting with the marinade. Barbecue the bananas in their skins alongside the chicken. Serve the bananas split open with a teaspoon of mango relish.

Skewered Chicken with Bramble Sauce

This fall recipe can be made with fresh-picked wild blackberries from the hedgerow if you're lucky enough to have a good supply.

Serves 4

INGREDIENTS

4 chicken breasts or 8 thighs
4 tbsp dry white wine or cider
2 tbsp chopped fresh rosemary
pepper

rosemary sprigs
   and blackberries, to garnish
green salad, to serve

SAUCE:
scant 2 cups blackberries
1 tbsp cider vinegar
2 tbsp redcurrant jelly
$1/4$ tsp grated nutmeg

1 Using a sharp knife, cut the chicken into 1 inch pieces and place in a bowl. Sprinkle over the white wine and rosemary, and season well with pepper. Cover and leave to marinate for at least an hour.

2 Drain the chicken, reserving the marinade, and thread the meat on to 8 skewers.

3 Cook on a preheated moderately hot broiler for 8–10 minutes, turning, until golden and evenly cooked.

4 Meanwhile, to make the sauce, place the marinade in a pan with the blackberries and simmer gently until soft. Press the mixture though a strainer using the back of a spoon.

5 Return the blackberry purée to the pan with the cider vinegar and redcurrant jelly and bring to a boil. Boil uncovered until the sauce is reduced by about one-third.

6 Spoon a little bramble sauce onto each plate and place a

chicken skewer on top. Sprinkle with nutmeg and serve hot. Garnish with rosemary and blackberries and serve.

COOK'S TIP

If you use canned fruit, omit the redcurrant jelly.

Sesame Chicken Brochettes with Cranberry Sauce

The cranberries give the sauce a lovely tart flavor. It can be served hot or cold.

Serves 8

INGREDIENTS

4 chicken breasts, skinned and boned
4 tbsp dry white wine
1 tbsp light muscovado sugar
2 tbsp sunflower oil
3^1/$_2$ oz sesame seeds
salt and pepper

TO SERVE:
boiled new potatoes
green salad leaves

SAUCE:
6 oz cranberries
^{2}/$_3$ cup cranberry juice drink
2 tbsp light muscovado sugar

1 Cut the chicken into 1 inch pieces. Put the wine, sugar, oil, and salt and pepper to taste in a large bowl, stirring to combine. Add the chicken pieces and toss to coat. Leave to marinate for at least 30 minutes, turning the chicken occasionally.

2 To make the sauce, place the ingredients in a small saucepan and bring slowly to a boil, stirring. Simmer gently for 5–10 minutes until the cranberries are soft and pulpy. Taste and add a little extra sugar if wished. Keep warm or leave to chill as required.

3 Remove the chicken pieces from the marinade with a draining spoon. Thread the chicken pieces on to 8 skewers, spacing them slightly apart to ensure even cooking.

4 Barbecue on an oiled rack over hot coals for 4–5 minutes on each side until just cooked. Brush several times with the marinade during cooking.

5 Remove the chicken skewers from the rack and roll in the sesame seeds. Return to the barbecue and cook for about 1 minute on each side or until the sesame seeds are toasted. Serve with the cranberry sauce, new potatoes, and salad greens.

VARIATION

Cranberry sauce goes well with all types of poultry. Try it with turkey or guinea fowl.

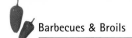

Tropical Chicken Skewers

In this recipe, chicken is given a Caribbean flavor. The marinade keeps them moist and succulent during cooking.

Serves 6

INGREDIENTS

1 lb 10 oz boneless
   chicken breasts
2 tbsp medium sherry

3 mangoes
bay leaves
2 tbsp oil

2 tbsp coarsely shredded coconut
pepper

1 Remove the skin from the chicken and cut into 1 inch cubes and toss in the sherry, with a little pepper.

2 Using a sharp knife, cut the mangoes into 1 inch cubes, discarding the stone and skin.

3 Thread the chicken, mango cubes, and bay leaves alternately onto long skewers, then brush lightly with oil.

4 Broil the skewers on a preheated moderately hot broiler for about 8–10 minutes, turning occasionally until golden.

5 Sprinkle the skewers with the coconut and broil for a further 30 seconds. Serve with a crisp salad.

COOK'S TIP

Use mangoes that are ripe but still firm so that they hold together on the skewers during cooking. Another firm fruit that would be suitable is pineapple.

COOK'S TIP

Remember that if you are using metal skewers, they will get very hot, so be sure to use gloves or tongs to turn them. Wooden skewers should be soaked in water for 30 minutes before use to prevent them from burning on the barbecue, and the exposed ends should be covered with pieces of kitchen foil.

Chicken Satay

This is an ideal sauce to accompany food cooked on the grill,
and it can be kept warm at the side of the rack.

Serves 4

INGREDIENTS

2 chicken breasts, skinned and boned

MARINADE:
4 tbsp sunflower oil
2 cloves garlic minced
3 tbsp fresh, chopped cilantro
1 tbsp superfine sugar
$1/2$ tsp ground cumin

$1/2$ tsp ground coriander
1 tbsp soy sauce
1 red or green chili, seeded
salt and pepper

SAUCE:
2 tbsp sunflower oil
1 small onion, chopped finely

1 red or green chili, seeded and
chopped
$1/2$ tsp ground coriander
$1/2$ tsp ground cumin
8 tbsp peanut butter
8 tbsp chicken stock or water
1 tbsp block coconut

1 Soak 8 wooden skewers in large, shallow dish of cold water for at least 30 minutes. This process will prevent the skewers from burning during grilling.

2 Cut the chicken lengthwise into 8 long strips. Thread the strips of chicken, concertina-style, onto the skewers and set aside while you make the marinade.

3 Place the ingredients for the marinade in a food processor and process until smooth.

4 Coat the chicken with the marinade paste, cover, and leave to chill in the refrigerator for at least 2 hours.

5 To make the sauce, heat the oil in a small pan and fry the onion and chili until they are

softened but not browned. Stir in the spices and cook for 1 minute. Add the remaining sauce ingredients and cook the mixture gently for 5 minutes. Keep warm at the side of the grill.

6 Grill the chicken skewers over hot coals for about 10 minutes, basting with any remaining marinade. Serve with the warm sauce.

Thai-Style Chicken Skewers

Here the chicken is marinated in a delicious aromatic sauce
before being threaded onto skewers.

Serves 4

INGREDIENTS

4 chicken breasts, skinned and boned
1 onion, peeled and cut into wedges
1 large red bell pepper, seeded
1 large yellow bell pepper, seeded

12 kaffir lime leaves
2 tbsp sunflower oil
2 tbsp lime juice
tomato halves, to serve

MARINADE:
1 tbsp Thai red curry paste
$^2/_3$ cup canned coconut milk

1 To make the marinade, place the red curry paste in a small pan over medium heat and cook for 1 minute. Add half of the coconut milk to the pan and bring the mixture to a boil. Boil for 2–3 minutes until the liquid has reduced by about two-thirds.

2 Remove the pan from the heat and stir in the remaining coconut milk. Set aside to cool.

3 Cut the chicken into 1 inch pieces. Stir the chicken into the cold marinade, cover, and leave to chill for at least 2 hours.

4 Cut the onion into wedges and the bell peppers into 1 inch pieces.

5 Remove the chicken pieces from the marinade and thread them onto skewers, alternating chicken with the vegetables and lime leaves.

6 Combine the oil and lime juice in a small bowl and brush the mixture over the kabobs. Barbecue the skewers over hot coals, turning and basting frequently for 10–15 minutes until the chicken is cooked through.

Barbecue the tomato halves and serve with the chicken skewers.

COOK'S TIP

Cooking the marinade first intensifies the flavor. It is important to allow the marinade to cool before adding the chicken, or bacteria may breed in the warm temperature. You will find fresh kaffir lime leaves in oriental stores, but if these are unavailable, bay leaves can be used instead.

Chicken Tikka Skewers

Traditionally, chicken tikka is cooked in a clay tandoori oven, but it works well on the barbecue too.

Makes 6

INGREDIENTS

4 chicken breasts, skinned and boned
$1/2$ tsp salt
4 tbsp lemon or lime juice

MARINADE:
$2/3$ cup unsweetened yogurt
2 cloves garlic, minced

1 inch piece gingerroot, peeled and grated
1 tsp ground cumin
1 tsp chili powder
$1/2$ tsp ground coriander
$1/2$ tsp ground turmeric
oil or melted butter for brushing

SAUCE:
$2/3$ cup unsweetened yogurt
1 tsp mint sauce

1 Cut the chicken into 1 inch cubes. Sprinkle with the salt and the lemon or lime juice and leave to stand for about 10 minutes.

2 To make the marinade, combine the yogurt, garlic, ginger, and ground spices together in a small bowl until well mixed.

3 Thread the cubes of chicken onto skewers. Brush the marinade over the chicken. Cover and leave to marinate in the refrigerator for at least 2 hours, preferably overnight.

4 Barbecue the chicken skewers over hot coals, brushing with oil or butter and turning frequently, for about 15 minutes or until cooked through.

5 Meanwhile, combine the yogurt and mint to make the sauce. Serve the chicken skewers with the mint and yogurt sauce.

VARIATION

Use the marinade to coat chicken portions, such as drumsticks, rather than cubes of chicken, if you prefer. Barbecue over medium hot coals for 30–40 minutes, until the juices run clear when the chicken is pierced with a skewer.

Dinner Party Dishes

Because chicken is popular throughout the world, there are countless spicy recipes from Asia, Mexico, the Caribbean, Spain, and Japan. Lime juice, peanut, coconut, and chili add the authentic tastes of Thailand to Chili Coconut Chicken, while Kashmiri Chicken is a rich and spicy dish from Northern India with an aromatic sauce made from yogurt, Tikka curry paste, cumin, ginger, chili, and almonds. From Spain comes Spanish Chicken with Shrimp, with its unusual mixture of chicken and shellfish together with the famous spicy Spanish sausage, chorizo, slow-cooked in a sauce of garlic, tomatoes, and white wine. Cumin-Spiced Apricot Chicken is a creative modern dish that would be perfect for any special occasion. The chicken is stuffed with dried apricots, coated in a yogurt, cumin, and turmeric sauce and served with nutty rice. There is even a dish from Japan, Teppanyaki, a simple dish of fried chicken slices with bell peppers, scallions, and beansprouts, served with a Mirin dipping sauce.

Prosciutto-Wrapped Chicken

There is a delicious surprise inside these chicken breast packets!

Serves 4

INGREDIENTS

4 chicken breasts, skin removed
3 1/2 oz full fat soft cheese, flavored
with herbs and garlic

8 slices prosciutto
2/3 cup red wine

2/3 cup chicken stock
1 tbsp brown sugar

1 Using a sharp knife, make a horizontal slit along the length of each chicken breast to form a packet.

2 Beat the cheese with a wooden spoon to soften it. Spoon the cheese into the pocket of the chicken breasts.

3 Wrap 2 slices of prosciutto around each chicken breast and secure with a piece of string.

4 Pour the wine and chicken stock into a large skillet and bring to a boil. When the mixture is just starting to boil, add the sugar and stir to dissolve.

5 Add the chicken breasts to the mixture in the skillet. Leave to simmer for 12–15 minutes or the chicken is tender and the juices run clear when a skewer is inserted into the thickest part of the meat.

6 Remove the chicken from the pan, set aside, and keep warm.

7 Reheat the sauce and boil until reduced and thickened. Remove the string from the chicken and cut into slices. Pour the sauce over the chicken to serve.

VARIATION

Try adding 2 finely chopped sun-dried tomatoes to the soft cheese in step 2, if you prefer.

Spanish Chicken with Shrimp

This unusual dish, with its mixture of chicken and shellfish, is typically Spanish. The basis of this recipe is sofrito: a slow-cooked mixture of onion and tomato in olive oil, with garlic and peppers.

Serves 4

INGREDIENTS

4 chicken quarters
1 tbsp olive oil
1 red bell pepper
1 medium onion
2 garlic cloves, minced

14 oz can chopped tomatoes
scant 1 cup dry white wine
4 tbsp chopped fresh oregano
1 cup chorizo sausage
1 cup peeled shrimp

salt and pepper
rice, to serve

1 Remove the skin from the chicken quarters. Heat the oil in a wide, heavy pan and fry the chicken, turning occasionally until golden brown.

2 Using a sharp knife, seed and slice the bell pepper and peel and slice the onion. Add the bell pepper and onion to the pan and fry gently to soften.

3 Add the garlic with the tomatoes, wine, and oregano.

Season well with salt and pepper, then bring to a boil, cover, and simmer gently for 45 minutes or until the chicken is tender and the juices run clear when the thickest part of the chicken is pierced with a skewer.

4 Thinly slice the chorizo and add to the pan together with the shrimp, then simmer for a further 5 minutes. Adjust the seasoning to taste and serve with rice.

COOK'S TIP

Chorizo is a spicy Spanish sausage made with pork and a hot pepper such as cayenne or pimento. It is available from large supermarkets and specialist butchers.

Spicy Chicken Tortillas

Serve these easy-to-prepare tortillas to friends or as a special family supper.
The chicken filling has a mild, mellow spicy heat and a fresh salad makes a perfect accompaniment.

Serves 4

INGREDIENTS

2 tbsp oil
8 skinless, boneless chicken
   thighs, sliced
1 onion, chopped
2 garlic cloves, chopped
1 tsp cumin seeds, roughly crushed
2 large dried chilies, sliced

14 oz can tomatoes
14 oz can red kidney
   beans, drained
$^2/_3$ cup chicken stock
2 tsp sugar
salt and pepper
lime wedges, to garnish

TO SERVE:
1 large ripe avocado
1 lime
8 soft tortillas
1 cup thick yogurt

1 Heat the oil in a large skillet or wok, add the chicken, and fry for 3 minutes until golden. Add the onion and fry for 5 minutes, stirring until browned. Add the garlic, cumin, and chilies, with their seeds, and cook for about 1 minute.

2 Add the tomatoes, kidney beans, stock, sugar, and salt and pepper to taste. Bring to a boil, breaking up the tomatoes. Cover and simmer for 15 minutes.

Remove the lid and cook for 5 minutes, stirring occasionally until the sauce has thickened.

3 Halve the avocado, discard the stone, and scoop out the flesh on to a plate. Mash the avocado with a fork. Cut half of the lime into 8 thin wedges. Squeeze the juice from the remaining lime over the avocado.

4 Warm the tortillas following the instructions on the packet.

Put two tortillas on each serving plate, fill with the chicken mixture, and top with spoonfuls of avocado and yogurt. Garnish the tortillas with lime wedges.

VARIATION

For a vegetarian filling, replace the chicken with 14 oz canned pinto or cannellini beans and use vegetable stock instead of the chicken stock.

Cajun Chicken Gumbo

This complete main course is cooked in one saucepan for simplicity. If you're cooking for one, simply halve the ingredients; the cooking time should stay the same.

Serves 2

INGREDIENTS

1 tbsp sunflower oil
4 chicken thighs
1 small onion, diced
2 stalks celery, diced

1 small green bell pepper, diced
$^1/_2$ cup long grain rice
$1^1/_4$ cups chicken stock
1 small red chilli

9 oz okra
1 tbsp tomato paste
salt and pepper

1 Heat the oil in a wide pan and fry the chicken until golden. Remove the chicken from the pan using a draining spoon. Stir in the onion, celery, and bell pepper and fry for 1 minute. Pour off any excess fat.

2 Add the rice and fry, stirring briskly, for a further minute. Add the chicken stock and heat until boiling.

3 Thinly slice the chili and trim the okra. Add to the pan with the tomato paste. Season to taste.

4 Return the chicken to the pan and stir. Cover tightly and simmer gently for 15 minutes, or until the rice is tender, the chicken is thoroughly cooked and all the liquid absorbed. Stir occasionally and if the gumbo becomes too dry, add a little extra stock to moisten. Serve immediately.

COOK'S TIP

The whole chili makes the dish hot and spicy – if you prefer a milder flavor, discard the seeds of the chili.

VARIATION

You can replace the chicken with 9 oz peeled shrimp and 3 oz belly of pork, if desired. Slice the pork and fry in the oil before adding the onions, and add the shrimp 5 minutes before the end of cooking time.

Mexican Chicken

*Chili, tomatoes, and corn are typical ingredients
in a Mexican dish.*

Serves 4

INGREDIENTS

2 tbsp oil
8 chicken drumsticks
1 medium onion, finely chopped
1 tsp chili powder

1 tsp ground coriander
14 oz can chopped tomatoes
2 tbsp tomato paste
²/₃ cup frozen corn-on-the-cob
salt and pepper

rice and mixed bell pepper salad,
to serve

1 Heat the oil in a large skillet, add the chicken drumsticks, and cook over a medium heat until browned. Remove the drumsticks from the pan with a draining spoon and set aside.

2 Add the chopped onion to the pan and cook for 3–4 minutes until softened, stir in the chili powder and coriander, and cook for a few seconds, stirring briskly so the spices do not burn on the bottom of the pan. Add the chopped tomatoes with their juice, the tomato paste, and stir both well to incorporate.

3 Return the chicken drumsticks to the pan and simmer the casserole gently for 20 minutes until the chicken is tender and thoroughly cooked. Add the corn-on-the-cob and cook for a further 3–4 minutes. Season with salt and pepper to taste.

4 Serve the Mexican Chicken with rice and mixed bell pepper salad.

COOK'S TIP

Mexican dishes are not usually suitable for freezing because the strong flavors they contain, such as chili, intensify during freezing, and if left for too long, an unpleasant, musty flavor can develop.

Chili Chicken & Corn Meatballs

Tender chicken nuggets are served with a sweet and sour sauce.

Serves 4

INGREDIENTS

1 lb lean chicken, ground
4 scallions, trimmed and finely
   chopped
1 small red chili, seeded and finely
   chopped
1 inch piece gingerroot, finely
   chopped
3^1/$_2$ oz can corn-on-the-cob (no
   added sugar or salt), drained
salt and white pepper

TO SERVE:
boiled jasmine rice
chives, snipped

SAUCE:
^{2}/$_3$ cup fresh chicken stock
3^1/$_2$ oz cubed pineapple in natural
   juice, drained, with
    4 tbsp reserved juice
1 medium carrot, cut into thin strips

1 small red bell pepper, seeded and
   diced
1 small green bell pepper, seeded and
   diced
1 tbsp light soy sauce
2 tbsp rice vinegar
1 tbsp superfine sugar
1 tbsp tomato paste
2 tsp cornstarch mixed to a paste
   with 4 tsp cold water

1 To make the meatballs, place the chicken in a bowl and add the scallion, chili, ginger, seasoning, and corn. Mix together with your hands.

2 Divide the mixture into 16 portions and form each into a ball. Bring a saucepan of water to a boil. Arrange the meatballs on a

sheet of baking parchment in a steamer or large strainer, place over the water, cover, and steam for 10–12 minutes.

3 To make the sauce, pour the stock and pineapple juice into a saucepan and bring to a boil. Add the carrot and bell peppers, cover, and simmer for 5 minutes.

4 Stir in the remaining ingredients and heat through, stirring, until thickened. Season and set aside until required.

5 Drain the meatballs and transfer to a serving plate. Garnish with snipped chives and serve with boiled rice and the sauce (re-heated if necessary).

Caribbean Chicken

This exotic dish can be made with any cut of chicken, but drumsticks are best for quick and even cooking. Grated fresh coconut adds a delicious, tropical flavor.

Serves 4

INGREDIENTS

8 skinless chicken drumsticks
2 limes
1 tsp cayenne pepper
2 medium mangoes

1 tbsp sunflower oil
2 tbsp dark muscovado sugar
lime wedges and fresh parsley,
    to garnish

2 tbsp coarsely grated coconut
    (optional), to serve

1 With a sharp knife, slash the chicken drumsticks at intervals then place the chicken in a large bowl.

2 Grate the peel from the limes and set aside.

3 Squeeze the juice from the limes and sprinkle over the chicken with the cayenne pepper. Cover and chill in the refrigerator for at least two hours or overnight.

4 Peel the mangoes and chop in half. Discard the stone and cut the flesh into slices.

5 Drain the chicken drumsticks using a draining spoon and reserve the juice. Heat the oil in a wide heavy pan and sauté the chicken drumsticks, turning frequently, until golden. Stir in the marinade, lime peel, mango slices, and the dark muscovado sugar.

6 Cover the pan and simmer gently, stirring occasionally, for 15 minutes, or until the chicken juices run clear when pierced with a skewer. Sprinkle with grated coconut, if using, and garnish with lime wedges and fresh parsley.

VARIATION

When buying mangoes, bear in mind that the skin of ripe mangoes varies in color from green to pinky-red and the flesh from pale yellow to bright orange. Choose mangoes which yield to gentle pressure.

Chicken in Red Bell Pepper & Almond Sauce

This tasty chicken dish combines warm spices and almonds and is spiked with anise.

Serves 4

INGREDIENTS

2 tbsp butter

7 tbsp vegetable oil

4 skinless, boneless chicken breasts, cut into 2 inch x 1 inch pieces

1 medium onion, roughly chopped

1 inch piece fresh gingerroot

3 garlic cloves, peeled

$^1/_4$ cup blanched almonds

1 large red bell pepper, roughly chopped

1 tbsp ground cumin

2 tsp ground coriander

1 tsp ground turmeric

pinch cayenne pepper

$^1/_2$ tsp salt

$^2/_3$ cup water

3 star anise

2 tbsp lemon juice

pepper

slivered almonds, to garnish

rice, to serve

1 Heat the butter and 1 tablespoon of oil in a skillet, add the chicken pieces, and cook for 5 minutes until golden. Transfer the chicken pieces to a plate and keep warm until required.

2 Combine the onion, ginger, garlic, almonds, red bell pepper, cumin, coriander, turmeric, cayenne pepper, and salt in a food processor or liquidizer. Blend to form a smooth paste.

3 Heat the remaining oil in a large saucepan or deep skillet. Add the paste and fry for 10–12 minutes.

4 Add the chicken pieces, the water, star anise, lemon juice, and pepper. Cover, reduce the heat and simmer gently for 25 minutes or until the chicken is tender, stirring a few times during cooking.

5 Transfer the chicken to a serving dish, sprinkle with the slivered almonds and serve with individual rice molds.

Fruity Garlic Curried Chicken

Serve this fruity curry with mango chutney and naan bread, and top the curry with seedless grapes. Mangoes or pears make a good substitute for pineapple.

Serves 4–6

INGREDIENTS

1 tbsp oil
2 lb chicken meat, chopped
4 tbsp flour, seasoned
32 shallots, roughly chopped
4 garlic cloves,
   minced with a little olive oil
3 cooking apples, diced

1 pineapple, diced
$3/4$ cup golden raisins
1 tbsp clear honey
$1^1/4$ cups chicken stock
2 tbsp Worcestershire sauce
3 tbsp hot curry paste
$2/3$ cup soured cream

salt and pepper
orange slices, to garnish
rice, to serve

1 Heat the oil in a large skillet. Coat the meat in the seasoned flour and cook for about 4 minutes until it is browned all over. Transfer the chicken to a large deep casserole and keep warm until required.

2 Slowly fry the shallots, garlic, apples, pineapple, and golden raisins in the pan juices.

3 Add the honey, chicken stock, Worcestershire sauce, and hot curry paste. Season to taste with salt and pepper.

4 Pour the sauce over the chicken and cover the casserole with a lid or cooking foil.

5 Cook in the center of a preheated oven, 350°F, for about 2 hours. Stir in the soured cream and cook for a further 15 minutes. Serve the curry with rice, garnished with a slice of orange.

VARIATION

Coconut rice also makes an excellent accompaniment to this dish. Place 1 oz chopped creamed coconut, 1 cinnamon stick, $2^1/4$ cups water in a large saucepan and bring to a boil. Stir in $1^3/4$ cups basmati rice, cover, and simmer gently for 15 minutes until all the liquid has been absorbed. Remove the cinnamon stick before serving.

Chicken Korma

*Korma is a typically mild and aromatic curry. If you want to reduce the fat
in this recipe, use unsweetened yogurt instead of the cream.*

Serves 4-6

INGREDIENTS

1 lb 10 oz chicken meat,
    cut into cubes
1¼ cups heavy cream
½ tsp garam masala

KORMA PASTE:
2 garlic cloves
1 inch fresh gingerroot,
    coarsely chopped
⅓ cup blanched almonds
6 tbsp chicken stock
1 tsp ground cardamon
4 cloves, minced

1 tsp cinnamon
2 large onions, chopped
1 tsp coriander seeds
2 tsp ground cumin seeds
pinch cayenne
6 tbsp olive oil
salt and pepper
cilantro, to garnish

1 Place all the ingredients for the korma paste into a blender or food processor and blend together until a very smooth paste is formed.

2 Place the cubes of chicken in a bowl and pour over the korma paste. Stir to coat the chicken completely with the paste. Cover and chill in the refrigerator for 3 hours to allow the flavors to permeate the chicken.

3 Simmer the meat in a large saucepan for 25 minutes, adding a little chicken stock if the mixture becomes too dry.

4 Add the heavy cream and garam masala to the pan and simmer for a further 15 minutes. Allow the korma to stand for 10 minutes before serving. Garnish the chicken korma with fresh cilantro and serve with rice.

COOK'S TIP

Garam masala is the name given to the mixture of spices commonly used as a base in curries. It can be bought ready-mixed or you can prepare your own by grinding together 1 tsp cardamon seeds, 2 tsp cloves, 2 tbsp each cumin seeds, and coriander seeds, 3 inch piece cinnamon stick, 1 tbsp black peppercorns, and 1 dried red chili.

Regal Chicken with Cashew Nut Stuffing

Most of the flavorful stuffing is cooked separately from the chicken, only a small amount is added to the neck end.

Serves 4

INGREDIENTS

1 chicken, weighing about
  3 lb 5 oz
1 small onion, halved
2 tbsp butter, melted
1 tsp ground turmeric
1 tsp ground ginger
$1/2$ tsp cayenne
salt and pepper
fresh cilantro, to garnish

STUFFING:
2 tbsp oil
1 medium onion, chopped finely
$1/2$ medium red bell pepper,
  chopped finely
2 garlic cloves, minced
$1/2$ cup basmati rice

$1^1/2$ cups hot chicken stock
grated peel of $1/2$ lemon
$1/2$ tsp ground turmeric
$1/2$ tsp ground ginger
$1/2$ tsp ground coriander
pinch cayenne pepper
$1/2$ cup salted cashew nuts

1 To make the stuffing, heat the oil in a saucepan, add the onion, red bell pepper, and garlic, and cook gently for 4–5 minutes. Add the rice and stir to coat in the oil. Add the stock, bring to a boil, then simmer for 15 minutes until all the liquid is absorbed. Transfer to a bowl and add the remaining ingredients for the stuffing. Season well with pepper.

2 Place half the stuffing in the neck end of the chicken and secure with a toothpick. Put the halved onion into the cavity of the chicken. Spoon the rest of the rice stuffing into a greased ovenproof dish and cover with foil.

3 Place the chicken in a roasting pan. Prick all over avoiding the stuffed area. Mix the butter and spices, season, then brush over the chicken.

4 Roast in a preheated oven, 375°F, for 1 hour, basting from time to time. Place the dish of rice stuffing in the oven and continue cooking the chicken for 30 minutes. Remove the toothpick and serve the chicken with stuffing and gravy.

Golden Chicken Pilauf

This is a simple version of a creamy textured and mildly spiced Indian pilauf. Although there are lots of ingredients, there's very little preparation needed for this dish.

Serves 4

INGREDIENTS

4 tbsp butter
8 skinless, boneless chicken thighs, cut into large pieces
1 medium onion, sliced
1 tsp ground turmeric
1 tsp ground cinnamon
1 cup long grain rice
1³/4 cups unsweetened yogurt

¹/3 cup golden raisins
1 scant cup chicken stock
1 medium tomato, chopped
2 tbsp chopped fresh cilantro or parsley
2 tbsp toasted coconut
salt and pepper
fresh cilantro, to garnish

1 Heat the butter in a heavy or non-stick pan and fry the chicken with the onion for about 3 minutes.

2 Stir in the turmeric, cinnamon, rice, and seasoning and fry for 3 minutes.

3 Add the unsweetened yogurt, golden raisins, and chicken stock and mix well. Cover and simmer for 10 minutes, stirring occasionally until the rice is tender and all the stock has been absorbed. Add more stock if the mixture becomes too dry.

4 Stir in the chopped tomato and fresh cilantro or parsley.

5 Sprinkle the pilauf with the toasted coconut and garnish with fresh cilantro.

COOK'S TIP

Long-grain rice is the most widely available and the cheapest rice. Basmati, with its slender grains and aromatic flavor, is more expensive and should be used on special occasions if it is not affordable on a frequent basis. Rice, especially basmati, should be washed thoroughly under cold, running water before use.

Kashmiri Chicken

This warming, rich and spicy dish is based on the traditional cooking style of Northern India, using chicken on the bone.

Serves 4

INGREDIENTS

4 skinless chicken drumsticks
4 skinless chicken thighs
$^2/_3$ cup unsweetened yogurt
4 tbsp Tikka curry paste
2 tbsp sunflower oil
1 medium onion, sliced thinly

1 garlic clove, minced
1 tsp ground cumin
1 tsp finely chopped fresh gingerroot
$^1/_2$ tsp chili paste
4 tsp chicken stock

2 tbsp ground almonds
salt
fresh cilantro, to garnish

1 Slash the chicken fairly deeply at intervals with a sharp knife and place in a large bowl.

2 Mix together the unsweetened yogurt and curry paste and stir into the chicken, tossing to coat evenly. Cover and chill for at least 1 hour.

3 Heat the oil in a large pan and fry the onion and garlic for 4–5 minutes until softened but not browned.

4 Stir in the cumin, ginger, and chili paste and cook gently for 1 minute.

5 Add the chicken pieces and fry gently, turning from time to time, for about 10 minutes or until evenly browned. Stir in any remaining marinade with the stock and almonds.

6 Cover the pan and simmer gently for a further 15 minutes or until the chicken is completely cooked and tender.

7 Season to taste with a little salt. Garnish the chicken with cilantro and serve with pilauf rice, pickles, and poppadums.

VARIATION

If you prefer, use boneless chicken breasts instead of legs, and cut into large chunks for cooking.

Cumin-Spiced Apricot Chicken

Spiced chicken legs are partially boned and packed with dried apricots for an intense fruity flavor. A golden, spiced, low-fat yogurt coating keeps the chicken moist and tender.

Serves 4

INGREDIENTS

4 large, skinless chicken
   leg quarters
finely grated peel of 1 lemon
1 cup ready-to-eat
   dried apricots
1 tbsp ground cumin

1 tsp ground turmeric
$^1/_2$ cup low-fat unsweetened yogurt
salt and pepper

TO SERVE:
1$^1/_2$ cups brown rice
2 tbsp slivered hazelnuts
   or almonds, toasted
2 tbsp sunflower seeds, toasted
lemon wedges and a fresh salad

1 Remove any excess fat from the chicken legs.

2 Use a small sharp knife to carefully cut the flesh away from the thigh bone.

3 Scrape the meat away down as far as the knuckle. Grasp the thigh bone firmly and twist it to break it from the drumstick.

4 Open out the boned part of the chicken and sprinkle with lemon peel and pepper. Pack the dried apricots into each piece of chicken. Fold over to enclose, and secure with toothpicks.

5 Mix together the cumin, turmeric, yogurt, and salt and pepper, then brush this mixture over the chicken to coat evenly. Place the chicken in an ovenproof dish or roasting pan and bake in a preheated oven, 375°F, for about 35–40 minutes, or until the juices run clear, not pink, when the chicken is pierced through the thickest part with a skewer.

6 Meanwhile, cook the rice in boiling, lightly salted water until just tender, then drain well. Stir the hazelnuts and sunflower seeds into the rice. Serve the chicken with the nutty rice, lemon wedges, and a fresh salad.

Chicken with a Curried Yogurt Crust

A spicy, Indian-style coating is baked around lean chicken to give a full flavor.
Serve hot or cold with a tomato, cucumber, and cilantro relish.

Serves 4

INGREDIENTS

1 garlic clove, minced

1 inch piece gingerroot, finely
    chopped

1 fresh green chili, seeded and finely
    chopped

6 tbsp low-fat unsweetened yogurt

1 tbsp tomato paste

1 tsp ground turmeric

1 tsp garam masala

1 tbsp lime juice

4 boneless, skinless chicken breasts,
    each 4$\frac{1}{2}$ oz

salt and pepper

wedges of lime or lemon, to serve

RELISH:

4 medium tomatoes

$\frac{1}{4}$ cucumber

1 small red onion

2 tbsp fresh cilantro, chopped

1 Preheat the oven to 375°F. In a small bowl mix together the garlic, ginger, chili, yogurt, tomato paste, turmeric, garam masala, lime juice, and seasoning.

2 Wash and pat dry the chicken breasts and place them on a baking sheet. Brush the spicy yogurt mix over the chicken and bake for 30–35 minutes until the meat is tender and cooked through.

3 Meanwhile, make the relish. Finely chop the tomatoes, cucumber, and onion, and mix together with the cilantro. Season, cover and chill until required.

4 Drain the cooked chicken on kitchen paper and serve hot with the relish. Or allow to cool, chill for at least 1 hour, and serve sliced as part of a salad.

VARIATION

The spicy yogurt coating would work just as well if spread on a chunky white fish such as cod fillet. The cooking time should be reduced to 15–20 minutes.

Chicken Tikka

For this very popular dish, small pieces of chicken are marinated for a minimum of 3 hours in yogurt and spices.

Serves 6

INGREDIENTS

1 tsp fresh gingerroot, finely
   chopped
1 tsp fresh garlic, minced
$1/2$ tsp ground coriander
$1/2$ tsp ground cumin
1 tsp chili powder
3 tbsp yogurt

1 tsp salt
2 tbsp lemon juice
a few drops of red food coloring
   (optional)
1 tbsp tomato paste
3 lb 5 oz chicken breast
1 onion, sliced

3 tbsp oil

TO GARNISH:
6 lettuce leaves
1 lemon, cut into wedges

1 Blend together the ginger, garlic, ground coriander, ground cumin, and chili powder in a large mixing bowl.

2 Add the yogurt, salt, lemon juice, red food coloring (if using), and the tomato paste to the spice mixture.

3 Using a sharp knife, cut the chicken into pieces. Add the chicken to the spice mixture and toss to coat well. Leave to marinate for at least 3 hours, preferably overnight.

4 Arrange the onion in the bottom of a heatproof dish. Carefully drizzle half of the oil over the onions.

5 Arrange the marinated chicken pieces on top of the onions and cook under a pre-heated broiler, turning once and basting with the remaining oil, for 25-30 minutes.

6 Serve the chicken tikka on a bed of lettuce and garnish with the lemon wedges.

COOK'S TIP

Chicken Tikka can be served with shop-bought naan breads and chutney and Raita (a mixture of chopped garlic and cucumber with unsweetened yogurt).

Chicken Tossed in Black Pepper

Using black pepper instead of chili powder produces a milder curry. This recipe is basically a stir-fry and can be prepared in a short time. The dish goes well with fried corn and peas.

Serves 4–6

INGREDIENTS

8 chicken thighs
1 tsp fresh gingerroot, finely
   chopped
1 tsp fresh garlic, minced
1 tsp salt
1¹/₂ tsp pepper
²/₃ cup oil

1 green bell pepper, roughly sliced
²/₃ cup water
2 tbsp lemon juice

FRIED CORN & PEAS:
2 oz unsalted butter
8 oz frozen corn

8 oz frozen peas
¹/₂ tsp salt
¹/₂ tsp chili powder
1 tbsp lemon juice
fresh cilantro leaves,
   to garnish

1 Using a sharp knife, bone the chicken thighs, if you prefer.

2 Combine the ginger, garlic, salt, and coarsely ground black pepper in a mixing bowl.

3 Add the chicken pieces to the black pepper mixture and set aside until required.

4 Heat the oil in a large pan. Add the chicken pieces and stir-fry for 10 minutes.

5 Reduce the heat and add the green bell pepper and the water to the pan. Leave the mixture to simmer for 10 minutes, then sprinkle over the lemon juice.

6 Meanwhile, make the fried corn and peas. Melt the butter in a large skillet. Add the corn and peas and fry, stirring occasionally, for about 10 minutes. Add the salt and chili powder and fry for a further 5 minutes.

7 Sprinkle over the lemon juice and garnish with fresh cilantro leaves.

8 Transfer the chicken and bell pepper mixture to serving plates and serve with the fried corn and peas.

Chicken & Onions

This dish represents one of the rare occasions when we do not use yogurt to cook chicken.
It has a lovely flavor and is perfect served with rice. It also freezes very well.

Serves 4

INGREDIENTS

1¼ cups oil
4 medium onions, finely chopped
1½ tsp fresh gingerroot, finely
   chopped
1½ tsp garam masala
1½ tsp fresh garlic, minced

1 tsp chili powder
1 tsp ground coriander
3 whole cardamoms
3 peppercorns
3 tbsp tomato paste
8 chicken thighs, skinned

1¼ cups water
2 tbsp lemon juice
1 green chili
fresh cilantro leaves
green chili strips, to garnish

1 Heat the oil in a large skillet. Add the onion and fry, stirring occasionally, until golden brown.

2 Reduce the heat and add the ginger, garam masala, garlic, chili powder, ground coriander, whole cardamoms, and the peppercorns, stirring to mix.

3 Add the tomato paste to the mixture in the skillet and stir-fry for 5-7 minutes.

4 Add the chicken thighs to the pan and toss to coat with the spice mixture.

5 Pour the water into the saucepan, cover, and leave to simmer for 20-25 minutes.

6 Add the lemon juice, green chili, and cilantro to the mixture, and combine.

7 Transfer the chicken and onions to serving plates, garnish and serve hot.

COOK'S TIP

A dish of meat cooked with plenty of onions is called a Do Pyaza. *This curry definitely improves if made in advance and then reheated before serving. This develops the flavors and makes them deeper.*

Chicken Drumsticks Deep-Fried with Herbs & Spices

One of my favorite dinner-party dishes, this is very attractive to look at. It should ideally be cooked and served from a karahi, *but if you do not have one, a deep, heavy skillet will do.*

Serves 4

INGREDIENTS

8 chicken drumsticks
$1^{1}/_{2}$ tsp fresh gingerroot, finely chopped
$1^{1}/_{2}$ tsp fresh garlic, minced
1 tsp salt
2 medium onions, chopped

$^{1}/_{2}$ large bunch fresh cilantro leaves
4-6 green chilies
$2^{1}/_{2}$ cups oil
4 firm tomatoes, cut into wedges
2 large green bell peppers, roughly chopped

1 Make 2-3 slashes in each piece of chicken. Rub the ginger, garlic, and salt over the chicken pieces and set aside.

2 Place half of the onions, the cilantro leaves, and green chilies in a pestle and mortar and grind to a paste. Rub the paste over the chicken pieces.

3 Heat the oil in a *karahi* or large skillet. Add the remaining onions and fry until golden brown. Remove the onions from the pan with a draining spoon and set aside.

4 Reduce the heat to medium hot and fry the chicken pieces, in batches of about 2 at a time, until cooked through (about 5-7 minutes per piece).

5 When all of the chicken pieces are cooked through, remove them from the pan, keep warm and set aside.

6 Add the tomatoes and the bell peppers to the pan and half-cook them until they are softened but still have bite.

7 Transfer the tomatoes and bell peppers to a serving plate and arrange the chicken on top. Garnish with the reserved fried onions.

Buttered Chicken

A simple and mouth-watering dish with a lovely thick sauce,
this makes an impressive centerpiece for a dinner party.

Serves 4–6

INGREDIENTS

8 tbsp unsalted butter
1 tbsp oil
2 medium onions, finely chopped
1 tsp fresh gingerroot, finely
  chopped
2 tsp garam masala
2 tsp ground coriander
1 tsp chili powder

1 tsp black cumin seeds
1 tsp fresh garlic, minced
1 tsp salt
3 whole green cardamoms
3 whole black peppercorns
$^2/_3$ cup natural yogurt
2 tbsp tomato paste
8 chicken pieces, skinned

$^2/_3$ cup water
2 whole bay leaves
$^2/_3$ cup light cream

TO GARNISH:
fresh cilantro leaves
2 green chilies, chopped

1 Heat the butter and oil in a large skillet. Add the onions and fry until golden brown, stirring. Reduce the heat.

2 Crush the fresh ginger and place in a bowl. Add the garam masala, ground coriander, ginger, chili powder, black cumin seeds, garlic, salt, cardamoms, and black peppercorns, and blend. Add the yogurt and tomato paste and stir to combine.

3 Add the chicken pieces to the yogurt and spice mixture and mix to coat well.

4 Add the chicken to the onions in the pan and stir-fry vigorously, making semi-circular movements, for 5-7 minutes.

5 Add the water and the bay leaves to the mixture in the pan and leave to simmer for 30 minutes, stirring occasionally.

6 Add the cream and cook for a further 10-15 minutes.

7 Garnish with cilantro leaves and chilies and serve hot.

Tandoori-Style Chicken

In India, tandoori chicken is traditionally cooked in a clay oven. Alternatively, I pre-heat the broiler to a very high temperature then lower it to medium to cook this dish.

Serves 4

INGREDIENTS

8 chicken drumsticks, skinned
$^2/_3$ cup unsweetened yogurt
$1^1/_2$ tsp fresh gingerroot, finely chopped
$1^1/_2$ tsp fresh garlic, minced
1 tsp chili powder

2 tsp ground cumin
2 tsp ground coriander
1 tsp salt
$^1/_2$ tsp red food coloring
1 tbsp tamarind paste
$^2/_3$ cup water

$^2/_3$ cup oil
lettuce leaves, to serve
TO GARNISH:
onion rings
sliced tomatoes
lemon wedges

1 Make 2-3 slashes in each piece of chicken.

2 Place the yogurt in a bowl. Add the ginger, garlic, chili powder, ground cumin, ground coriander, salt, and red food coloring and blend together until well combined.

3 Add the chicken to the yogurt and spice mixture and mix to coat well. Leave the chicken to marinate in the refrigerator for a minimum of 3 hours.

4 In a separate bowl, mix the tamarind paste with the water and fold into the yogurt and spice mixture. Toss the chicken pieces in this mixture and set aside to marinate for a further 3 hours.

5 Transfer the chicken pieces to a heatproof dish and brush the chicken with oil. Cook the chicken under a pre-heated medium-hot broiler for 30-35 minutes, turning the chicken pieces occasionally and basting with the remaining oil.

6 Arrange the chicken on a bed of lettuce and garnish with onion rings, sliced tomatoes, and lemon wedges.

COOK'S TIP

Serve the succulent chicken pieces on a bed of lettuce, and garnished with a few onion rings, sliced tomatoes and lemon wedges. Shop-bought naan bread and Raita (see page 328) will complement the dish perfectly.

Spicy Roast Chicken

This chicken dish, ideal for dinner parties, is cooked in the oven – which is very rare in Indian cooking. The chicken can be boned, if desired.

Serves 4

INGREDIENTS

$^1/_4$ cup ground almonds
$^1/_3$ cup shredded coconut
$^2/_3$ cup oil
1 medium onion, finely chopped
1 tsp fresh gingerroot, chopped
1 tsp fresh garlic, minced

1 tsp chili powder
$1^1/_2$ tsp garam masala
1 tsp salt
$^2/_3$ cup yogurt
4 chicken quarters, skinned
green salad leaves, to serve

TO GARNISH:
fresh cilantro leaves
1 lemon, cut into wedges

1 In a heavy-based saucepan, dry roast the ground almonds and coconut and set aside.

2 Heat the oil in a skillet and fry the onion, stirring, until golden brown.

3 Place the ginger, garlic, chili powder, garam masala, and salt in a bowl and mix with the yogurt. Add the almonds and coconut and mix well.

4 Add the onions to the spice mixture, blend, and set aside.

5 Arrange the chicken quarters in the bottom of a heatproof dish. Spoon the spice mixture over the chicken sparingly.

6 Cook in a pre-heated oven, 425°F, for 35-45 minutes. Check that the chicken is cooked thoroughly by piercing the thickest part of the meat with a sharp knife or a fine skewer – the juices will run clear when the chicken is cooked through. Garnish with the cilantro and lemon wedges and serve with a salad.

COOK'S TIP

If you want a more spicy dish, add more chili powder and garam masala.

Chicken Jalfrezi

This is a quick and tasty way to use leftover roast chicken. The sauce can also be used for any cooked poultry, lamb, or beef.

Serves 4

INGREDIENTS

1 tsp mustard oil
3 tbsp vegetable oil
1 large onion, chopped finely
3 garlic cloves, minced
1 tbsp tomato paste
2 tomatoes, peeled and chopped
1 tsp ground turmeric

$^1/_2$ tsp cumin seeds, ground
$^1/_2$ tsp coriander seeds, ground
$^1/_2$ tsp chili powder
$^1/_2$ tsp garam masala
1 tsp red wine vinegar
1 small red bell pepper, chopped

1 cup frozen fava beans
1 lb cooked chicken breasts, cut into
   bite-sized pieces
salt
fresh cilantro sprigs, to garnish

1 Heat the mustard oil in a large skillet set over a high heat for about 1 minute until it begins to smoke. Add the vegetable oil, reduce the heat, and add the onion and the garlic. Fry the garlic and onion until golden.

2 Add the tomato paste, chopped tomatoes, ground turmeric, cumin and coriander seeds, chili powder, garam masala, and red wine vinegar to the skillet. Stir the mixture until fragrant.

3 Add the red bell pepper and fava beans and stir for 2 minutes until the bell pepper is softened. Stir in the chicken, and salt to taste. Leave to simmer gently for 6-8 minutes until the chicken is heated through and the beans are tender.

4 Serve garnished with cilantro leaves.

COOK'S TIP

This dish is an ideal way of making use of leftover poultry – turkey, duck, or quail. Any variety of beans works well, but vegetables are just as useful, especially root vegetables, zucchini, potatoes, or broccoli. Leafy vegetables will not be so successful.

Teppanyaki

This simple, Japanese style of cooking is ideal for thinly sliced breast of chicken. Mirin is a rich, sweet rice wine which is available from oriental shops.

Serves 4

INGREDIENTS

4 boneless chicken breasts
1 red bell pepper
1 green bell pepper
4 scallions

8 baby corn-on-the-cob
1/2 cup beansprouts
1 tbsp sesame or sunflower oil
4 tbsp soy sauce

4 tbsp mirin
1 tbsp grated fresh gingerroot

1 Remove the skin from the chicken and slice at a slight angle, to a thickness of 1/4 inch.

2 Seed and thinly slice the bell peppers and trim and slice the scallions and corn-on-the-cob. Arrange the bell peppers, scallions, corn, and beansprouts on a plate with the sliced chicken.

3 Heat a large griddle or heavy skillet then lightly brush with oil. Add the vegetables and chicken slices in small batches, allowing space between them so they cook thoroughly.

4 In a small bowl, mix together the soy sauce, mirin and ginger and serve as a dip with the chicken and vegetables.

VARIATION

If you cannot find mirin add one tablespoon of soft, light brown sugar to the sauce instead.

VARIATION

Instead of serving the sauce as a dip, you could use it as a marinade. However, do not leave it to marinate for more than 2 hours as the soy sauce will cause the chicken to dry out and become tough. Use other vegetables, such as snow peas or thinly sliced carrots, if you prefer.

Thai Stir-Fried Chicken with Vegetables

Coconut adds a creamy texture and delicious flavor to this Thai-style stir-fry, which is spiked with green chili.

Serves 4

INGREDIENTS

3 tbsp sesame oil
12 oz chicken breast,
    sliced thinly
8 shallots, sliced
2 garlic cloves, finely chopped

1 inch piece fresh
    gingerroot, grated
1 green chili, finely chopped
1 each red and green bell pepper,
    sliced thinly
3 zucchini, thinly sliced

2 tbsp ground almonds
1 tsp ground cinnamon
1 tbsp oyster sauce
$^1/_4$ cup creamed
    coconut, grated
salt and pepper

1 Heat the sesame oil in a wok, add the chicken, season with salt and pepper, and stir fry for about 4 minutes.

2 Add the shallots, garlic, ginger, and chili and stir-fry for 2 minutes.

3 Add the bell peppers and zucchini and cook for about 1 minute.

4 Finally, add the remaining ingredients and seasoning. Stir-fry for 1 minute and serve.

COOK'S TIP

Creamed coconut is sold in blocks by supermarkets and oriental stores. It is a useful store-cupboard standby as it adds richness and depth of flavor.

COOK'S TIP

Since most of the heat of chilies comes from the seeds, remove them before cooking if you want a milder flavor. Be very careful when handling chilies – do not touch your face or eyes as the chili juice can be very painful. Always wash your hands after preparing chilies.

Chili Chicken

*This is quite a hot dish, using fresh chilies. If you prefer
a milder dish, halve the number of chilies used.*

Serves 4

INGREDIENTS

12 oz skinless, boneless
   lean chicken
$^1/_2$ tsp salt
1 egg white, lightly beaten
2 tbsp cornstarch
4 tbsp vegetable oil

2 garlic cloves, minced
$^1/_2$-inch piece fresh gingerroot,
   grated
1 red bell pepper, seeded and diced
1 green bell pepper, seeded
   and diced

2 fresh red chilies, chopped
2 tbsp light soy sauce
1 tbsp dry sherry or Chinese rice wine
1 tbsp wine vinegar

1 Cut the chicken into cubes and place in a mixing bowl. Add the salt, egg white, cornstarch, and 1 tablespoon of the oil. Turn the chicken in the mixture to coat thoroughly.

2 Heat the remaining oil in a preheated wok. Add the garlic and ginger and stir-fry for 30 seconds.

3 Add the chicken pieces to the wok and stir-fry for 2–3 minutes, or until browned.

4 Stir in the bell peppers, chilies, soy sauce, sherry or Chinese rice wine, and wine vinegar and cook for a further 2–3 minutes, until the chicken is cooked through. Transfer to a warm serving dish and serve.

VARIATION

*This recipe works well if you use
12 oz lean steak, cut into thin strips
or 1 lb raw shrimp instead of
the chicken.*

COOK'S TIP

*When preparing chilies, wear
rubber gloves to prevent the juices
from burning and irritating your
hands. Be careful not to touch your
face, especially your lips or eyes,
until you have washed your hands.*

Chili Coconut Chicken

This tasty Thai-style dish has a classic sauce of lime, peanut, coconut, and chili.
You'll find coconut cream in most supermarkets or delicatessens.

Serves 4

INGREDIENTS

$2/3$ cup hot chicken stock

$1/3$ cup coconut cream

1 tbsp sunflower oil

8 skinless, boneless chicken thighs,
   cut into long, thin strips

1 small red chili, sliced thinly

4 scallions, sliced thinly

4 tbsp smooth or crunchy
   peanut butter

finely grated peel and juice of 1 lime

scallion flower and red chili, to
   garnish

boiled rice, to serve

1 Place the chicken stock in a measuring jug and crumble the creamed coconut into the stock, stirring to dissolve.

2 Heat the oil in a wok or large heavy skillet and cook the chicken strips, stirring, until golden.

3 Add the sliced red chili and the scallions to the pan and cook gently for a few minutes, stirring to mix all the ingredients.

4 Add the peanut butter, coconut cream, lime peel and juice, and simmer uncovered, stirring, for about 5 minutes.

5 Serve with boiled rice, garnished with a scallion flower and a red chili.

VARIATION

Serve jasmine rice with this spicy dish. It has a fragrant aroma that is well-suited to Thai-style recipes.

VARIATION

Limes are used frequently in Thai cookery, particularly in conjunction with sweet flavors such as coconut or peanut. They are used in preference to lemons because they have a more acidic flavor which lends freshness and tartness to many dishes. If limes are unavailable, you can use lemons instead.

Chicken with Bell Peppers & Black Bean Sauce

This tasty chicken stir-fry is quick and easy to make and is full of fresh flavors and crunchy vegetables.

Serves 4

INGREDIENTS

14 oz chicken breasts,
   sliced thinly
pinch of cornstarch
2 tbsp oil
1 garlic clove, minced
1 tbsp black bean sauce
1 each small red and green bell
   pepper, cut into strips

1 red chili, chopped finely
1 cup mushrooms, sliced
1 onion, chopped
6 scallions, chopped
salt and pepper
fresh noodles, to serve

SEASONING:
$^{1}/_{2}$ tsp salt
$^{1}/_{2}$ tsp sugar
3 tbsp chicken stock
1 tbsp dark soy sauce
2 tbsp beef stock
2 tbsp rice wine
1 tsp cornstarch, blended with a little
   rice wine

1   Put the chicken strips in a bowl. Add a pinch of salt and a pinch of cornstarch and cover with water. Leave for 30 minutes.

2   Heat 1 tbsp of the oil in a wok or deep-sided skillet and stir-fry the chicken for 4 minutes. Transfer the chicken to a warm serving dish and clean the wok or pan.

3   Add the remaining oil to the wok and add the garlic, black bean sauce, green and red bell peppers, chili, mushrooms, onion, and scallions. Stir-fry the vegetables for 2 minutes then return the chicken to the wok.

4   Add the seasoning, fry for 3 minutes, and thicken with a little of the cornstarch paste. Serve.

COOK'S TIP

Black bean sauce can be found in specialist shops and in many supermarkets. Use dried noodles if you can't find fresh noodles.

Chicken with Yellow Bean Sauce

*Ready-made yellow bean sauce is available from large supermarkets and Chinese food stores.
It is made from yellow soya beans and is quite salty in flavor.*

Serves 4

INGREDIENTS

1 lb skinless, boneless
   chicken breasts
1 egg white, beaten
1 tbsp cornstarch
1 tbsp rice wine vinegar
1 tbsp light soy sauce

1 tsp superfine sugar
3 tbsp vegetable oil
1 garlic clove, minced
$1/2$-inch piece gingerroot, grated

1 green bell pepper, seeded
   and diced
2 large mushrooms, sliced
3 tbsp yellow bean sauce
yellow or green bell pepper strips,
   to garnish

1 Trim any fat from the chicken and cut into 1-inch cubes.

2 Mix the egg white and cornstarch in a shallow bowl. Add the chicken and turn in the mixture to coat. Set aside for 20 minutes.

3 Mix the vinegar, soy sauce, and sugar in a bowl.

4 Remove the chicken from the egg white mixture.

5 Heat the oil in a preheated wok, add the chicken and stir-fry for 3–4 minutes, until golden brown. Remove the chicken from the wok with a draining spoon, set aside and keep warm.

6 Add the garlic, ginger, bell pepper, and mushrooms and stir-fry for 1–2 minutes.

7 Add the yellow bean sauce and cook for 1 minute. Stir in the vinegar mixture and return the chicken to the wok. Cook for 1–2

minutes and serve hot, garnished with bell pepper strips.

VARIATION

Black bean sauce would work equally well with this recipe. Although this would affect the appearance of the dish, as it is much darker in color, the flavors would be compatible.

Crispy Chicken

In this recipe, the chicken is brushed with a syrup and deep-fried until golden.
It is a little time consuming, but well worth the effort.

Serves 4

INGREDIENTS

3 lb 5 oz oven-ready chicken
2 tbsp honey
2 tsp Chinese five-spice powder

2 tbsp rice wine vinegar
3 ³/4 cups vegetable oil, for frying
chili sauce, to serve

1 Rinse the chicken inside and out under cold running water and pat dry with paper towels.

2 Bring a large saucepan of water to a boil and remove from the heat. Place the chicken in the water, cover, and set aside for 20 minutes. Remove the chicken from the water and pat dry with paper towels. Cool and leave to chill in the refrigerator overnight.

3 To make the glaze, mix the honey, Chinese five-spice powder, and rice wine vinegar.

4 Brush some of the glaze all over the chicken and return to the refrigerator for 20 minutes. Repeat this process until all of the glaze has been used up. Return the chicken to the refrigerator for at least 2 hours after the final coating.

5 Using a cleaver or heavy kitchen knife, open the chicken out by splitting it through the center of the breast and then cut each half into 4 pieces.

6 Heat the oil for deep-frying in a wok until almost smoking. Reduce the heat and fry each piece of chicken for 5–7 minutes, until golden and cooked through. Remove from the oil with a draining spoon and drain on absorbent paper towels.

7 Transfer to a serving dish and serve hot with chili sauce.

COOK'S TIP

If it is easier, use chicken portions instead of a whole chicken. You could also use chicken legs for this recipe, if you prefer.

Spicy Peanut Chicken

This quick dish has many variations, but this version includes the classic combination of peanuts, chicken, and chilies, blending together to give a wonderfully flavored dish.

Serves 4

INGREDIENTS

$10^1/2$ oz skinless, boneless chicken
  breast
2 tbsp peanut oil
1 cup shelled peanuts
1 fresh red chili, sliced
1 green bell pepper, seeded and cut
  into strips

fried rice, to serve

SAUCE:
$2/3$ cup chicken stock
1 tbsp Chinese rice wine or
  dry sherry
1 tbsp light soy sauce

$1^1/2$ tsp light brown sugar
2 garlic cloves, minced
1 tsp grated fresh gingerroot
1 tsp rice wine vinegar
1 tsp sesame oil

1 Trim any fat from the chicken and cut the meat into 1-inch cubes. Set aside.

2 Heat the peanut oil in a preheated wok. Add the peanuts and stir-fry for 1 minute. Remove the peanuts with a draining spoon and set aside.

3 Add the chicken to the wok and cook for 1–2 minutes. Stir in the chili and green bell pepper and cook for 1 minute.

Remove from the wok with a draining spoon and set aside.

4 Put half of the peanuts in a food processor and process until almost smooth. Alternatively, place them in a plastic bag and crush them with a rolling pin.

5 To make the sauce, add the chicken stock, Chinese rice wine or dry sherry, soy sauce, sugar, garlic, ginger, and rice wine vinegar to the wok.

6 Heat the sauce without boiling and stir in the peanuts, chicken, chili, and bell pepper.

7 Sprinkle the sesame oil into the wok, stir, and cook for 1 minute. Serve hot with fried rice.

COOK'S TIP

If necessary, process the peanuts with a little of the stock in step 4 to form a softer paste.

Lemon Chicken

This is on everyone's list of favorite Chinese dishes, and it is so simple to make. Fried chicken is cooked in a tangy lemon sauce in minutes and is great served with stir-fried vegetables.

Serves 4

INGREDIENTS

vegetable oil, for deep-frying
1¹/₂ lb skinless, boneless chicken, cut
    into strips
lemon slices and shredded scallion,
    to garnish

SAUCE:
1 tbsp cornstarch
6 tbsp cold water
3 tbsp fresh lemon juice

2 tbsp sweet sherry
¹/₂ tsp superfine sugar

1 Heat the oil in a preheated wok until almost smoking. Reduce the heat and stir-fry the chicken strips for 3–4 minutes, until cooked through. Remove the chicken with a draining spoon, set aside, and keep warm. Drain the oil from the wok.

2 To make the sauce, mix the cornflour with 2 tablespoons of the water to form a paste.

3 Pour the lemon juice and remaining water into the mixture in the wok. Add the sherry and sugar and bring to a boil, stirring until the sugar has completely dissolved.

4 Stir in the cornflour mixture and return to a boil. Reduce the heat and simmer, stirring constantly, for 2-3 minutes, until the sauce is thickened and clear.

5 Transfer the chicken to a warm serving plate and pour the sauce over the top. Garnish with the lemon slices and shredded scallion and serve immediately.

COOK'S TIP

If you would prefer to use chicken portions rather than strips, cook them in the oil, covered, over a low heat for about 30 minutes, or until cooked through.

Braised Chicken

This is a delicious way to cook a whole chicken. It has a wonderful glaze, which is served as a sauce.

Serves 4

INGREDIENTS

3 lb 5 oz chicken
3 tbsp vegetable oil
1 tbsp peanut oil
2 tbsp dark brown sugar

5 tbsp dark soy sauce
$^2/_3$ cup water
2 garlic cloves, minced
1 small onion, chopped

1 fresh red chili, chopped
celery leaves and chives, to garnish

1 Clean the chicken inside and out with damp paper towels.

2 Put the oil in a large wok, add the sugar, and heat gently until the sugar caramelizes. Stir in the soy sauce. Add the chicken and turn it in the mixture to coat thoroughly on all sides.

3 Add the water, garlic, onion, and chili. Cover and simmer, turning the chicken, for about 1 hour, or until cooked through. Test by piercing a thigh with the point of a knife – the juices run clear when the chicken is done.

4 Remove the chicken from the wok and set aside. Increase the heat and reduce the sauce in the wok until thickened. Transfer the chicken to a serving plate, garnish with celery leaves and chives, and serve with the sauce.

COOK'S TIP

When caramelizing the sugar, do not turn the heat too high, otherwise it may burn.

VARIATION

For a spicier sauce, add 1 tbsp finely chopped fresh gingerroot and 1 tbsp ground Szechuan peppercorns with the chili in step 3. If the flavor of dark soy sauce is too strong for your taste, substitute 2 tbsp dark soy sauce and 3 tbsp light soy sauce. This will result in a more delicate taste without sacrificing the attractive color of the dish.

Chicken on Crispy Noodles

Blanched noodles are fried in the wok until crisp and brown, and then topped with a shredded chicken sauce for a delightfully tasty dish.

Serves 4

INGREDIENTS

8 oz skinless, boneless chicken
   breasts, shredded
1 egg white
5 tsp cornstarch
8 oz thin egg noodles

1²/₃ cups vegetable oil
2¹/₂ cups chicken stock
2 tbsp dry sherry
2 tbsp oyster sauce
1 tbsp light soy sauce

1 tbsp hoisin sauce
1 red bell pepper, seeded and very
   thinly sliced
2 tbsp water
3 scallions, chopped

1 Mix the chicken, egg white and 2 teaspoons of the cornstarch in a bowl. Let stand for at least 30 minutes.

2 Blanch the noodles in boiling water for 2 minutes, then drain thoroughly. Heat ¹/₂ of the oil in a preheated wok. Add the noodles, spreading them to cover the base of the wok. Cook over a low heat for about 5 minutes, until the noodles are browned on the underside. Flip the noodles over and brown on the other side.

Remove from the wok when crisp and browned, place on a serving plate, and keep warm. Drain the oil from the wok.

3 Add 1¹/₄ cups of the chicken stock to the wok. Remove from the heat and add the chicken, stirring well so that it does not stick. Return to the heat and cook for 2 minutes. Drain, discarding the stock.

4 Wipe the wok with paper towels and return to the heat.

Add the sherry, oyster sauce, soy sauce, hoisin sauce, red bell pepper, and the remaining chicken stock and bring to a boil. Blend the remaining cornstarch with the water to form a paste and stir it into the mixture.

5 Return the chicken to the wok and cook over a low heat for 2 minutes. Place the chicken on top of the noodles and sprinkle with scallions. Serve immediately.

Chicken & Rice Casserole

This is a spicy casserole of rice, chicken, vegetables, and chili in a soy and ginger flavored liquor.
Although called a casserole, the dish only requires approximately 30 minutes cooking time.

Serves 4

INGREDIENTS

$^2/_3$ cup long-grain rice
1 tbsp dry sherry
2 tbsp light soy sauce
2 tbsp dark soy sauce
2 tsp dark brown sugar
1 tsp salt

1 tsp sesame oil
2 lb skinless, boneless chicken meat, diced
$3^3/_4$ cups chicken stock
2 open-cap mushrooms, sliced
2 oz water chestnuts, halved

3 oz broccoli flowerets
1 yellow bell pepper, sliced
4 tsp grated fresh gingerroot
whole chives, to garnish

1 Cook the rice in a saucepan of boiling water for about 15 minutes. Drain well, rinse under cold water, and drain again thoroughly.

2 Place the sherry, soy sauce, sugar, salt, and sesame oil in a large bowl and mix together until well combined.

3 Stir the chicken into the soy mixture, turning to coat well. Leave to marinate for about 30 minutes.

4 Bring the stock to a boil in a saucepan or preheated wok.

5 Add the chicken with the marinade, mushrooms, water chestnuts, broccoli, bell pepper, and ginger.

6 Stir in the rice, reduce the heat, cover, and cook for 25-30 minutes, until the chicken and vegetables are cooked through.

7 Transfer to serving plates, garnish with chives and serve.

VARIATION

This dish would work equally well with beef or pork. Chinese dried mushrooms may be used instead of the open-cap mushrooms, if rehydrated before adding to the dish.

Chinese Chicken Rice

*This is a really colorful main meal or side dish
that tastes just as good as it looks.*

Serves 4

INGREDIENTS

1³/₄ cups long-grain white rice
1 tsp turmeric
2 tbsp sunflower oil
12 oz skinless, boneless chicken
    breasts or thighs, sliced
1 red bell pepper, seeded and sliced

1 green bell pepper, seeded and sliced
1 green chili, seeded and finely
    chopped
1 medium carrot, coarsely grated
1¹/₂ cups beansprouts

6 scallions, sliced, plus extra to
    garnish
2 tbsp soy sauce

1 Place the rice and turmeric in a large saucepan of lightly salted water and cook until the grains of rice are just tender, about 10 minutes. Drain the rice thoroughly and press out any excess water with double thickness paper towels.

2 Heat the sunflower oil in a large preheated wok.

3 Add the strips of chicken to the wok and stir-fry over a high heat until the chicken is just beginning to turn a golden color.

4 Add the bell peppers and chili to the wok and stir-fry for 2–3 minutes.

5 Add the rice to the wok, a little at a time, tossing well after each addition until well combined.

6 Add the carrot, beansprouts, and scallions to the wok and stir-fry for a further 2 minutes.

7 Drizzle with the soy sauce and mix well.

8 Garnish with extra scallions, if wished and serve at once.

VARIATION

*Use pork marinated in hoisin
sauce instead of the chicken,
if you prefer.*

Stir-Fried Onion Rice with Five-Spice Chicken

This dish has a wonderful color obtained from the turmeric, and a great spicy flavor, making it very appealing all round.

Serves 4

INGREDIENTS

1 tbsp Chinese five-spice powder
2 tbsp cornstarch
12 oz boneless, skinless chicken
   breasts, cubed

3 tbsp peanut oil
1 onion, diced
1 cup long-grain white rice
$^{1}/_{2}$ tsp turmeric

$2^{1}/_{2}$ cups chicken stock
2 tbsp snipped fresh chives

1   Place the Chinese five-spice powder and cornstarch in a large bowl. Add the chicken pieces and toss to coat all over.

2   Heat 2 tablespoons of the peanut oil in a large preheated wok. Add the chicken pieces to the wok and stir-fry for 5 minutes. Using a draining spoon, remove the chicken and set aside.

3   Add the remaining peanut oil to the wok.

4   Add the onion to the wok and stir-fry for 1 minute.

5   Add the rice, turmeric, and chicken stock to the wok and bring to a boil.

6   Return the chicken pieces to the wok, reduce the heat, and leave to simmer for 10 minutes, or until the liquid has been absorbed and the rice is tender.

7   Add the chives, stir to mix, and serve hot.

COOK'S TIP

Be careful when using turmeric as it can stain the hands and clothes a distinctive shade of yellow.

Chicken Chow Mein

This classic dish requires no introduction as it is already a favorite amongst most Chinese food-eaters and is familiar to almost everybody.

Serves 4

INGREDIENTS

9 oz packet of medium egg noodles

2 tbsp sunflower oil

9^1/$_2$ oz cooked chicken breasts, shredded

1 clove garlic, finely chopped

1 red bell pepper, seeded and thinly sliced

3^1/$_2$ oz shiitake mushrooms, sliced

6 scallions, sliced

1 cup beansprouts

3 tbsp soy sauce

1 tbsp sesame oil

1 Place the egg noodles in a large bowl or dish and break them up slightly.

2 Pour enough boiling water over the noodles to cover and leave to stand whilst preparing the other ingredients.

3 Heat the sunflower oil in a large preheated wok.

4 Add the shredded chicken, finely chopped garlic, bell pepper slices, mushrooms, scallions, and beansprouts to the wok and stir-fry for about 5 minutes.

5 Drain the noodles thoroughly. Add the noodles to the wok, toss well, and stir-fry for a further 5 minutes.

6 Drizzle the soy sauce and sesame oil over the chow mein and toss until well combined.

7 Transfer the chicken chow mein to warm serving bowls and serve immediately.

VARIATION

You can make the chow mein with a selection of vegetables for a vegetarian dish, if you prefer.

Egg Noodles with Chicken & Oyster Sauce

The chicken and noodles are cooked and then a flavored egg mixture is tossed into the dish to coat the noodles and meat in this delicious recipe.

Serves 4

INGREDIENTS

9 oz egg noodles
1 lb chicken thighs

2 tbsp peanut oil
3¹/₂ oz carrots, sliced

3tbsp oyster sauce
2 eggs
3 tbsp cold water

1 Place the egg noodles in a large bowl or dish. Pour enough boiling water over the noodles to cover and leave to stand for 10 minutes.

2 Meanwhile, remove the skin from the chicken thighs. Cut the chicken flesh into small pieces, using a sharp knife.

3 Heat the peanut oil in a large preheated wok.

4 Add the pieces of chicken and the carrot slices to the wok and stir-fry the mixture for about 5 minutes.

5 Drain the noodles thoroughly. Add the noodles to the wok and stir-fry for a further 2–3 minutes or until the noodles are heated through.

6 Beat together the oyster sauce, eggs and 3 tablespoons of cold water. Drizzle the mixture over the noodles and stir-fry for a further 2–3 minutes or until the eggs set. Transfer to warm serving bowls and serve hot.

VARIATION

Flavor the eggs with soy sauce or hoisin sauce as an alternative to the oyster sauce, if you prefer.

Creamy Chicken & Potato Casserole

Small new potatoes are ideal for this recipe as they can be cooked whole. If larger potatoes are used, cut them in half or into chunks before adding them to the casserole.

Serves 4

INGREDIENTS

2 tbsp vegetable oil
$^1/_4$ cup butter
4 chicken portions, about 8 oz each
2 leeks, sliced
1 garlic clove, minced
4 tbsp all-purpose flour

$3^3/_4$ cups chicken stock
$1^1/_4$ cups dry white wine
$4^1/_2$ oz baby carrots, halved lengthways

$4^1/_2$ oz baby corn-on-the-cobs, halved lengthways
1 lb small new potatoes
1 bouquet garni
$^2/_3$ cup heavy cream
salt and pepper

1 Heat the oil in a large skillet. Cook the chicken for 10 minutes, turning until browned all over. Transfer the chicken to a casserole dish using a draining spoon.

2 Add the leek and garlic to the skillet and cook for 2-3 minutes, stirring. Stir in the flour and cook for a further 1 minute. Remove the skillet from the heat and stir in the stock and wine. Season well.

3 Return the pan to the heat and bring the mixture to a boil. Stir in the carrots, corns, potatoes, and bouquet garni.

4 Transfer the mixture to the casserole dish. Cover and cook in a preheated oven, 350°F, for about 1 hour.

5 Remove the casserole from the oven and stir in the cream. Return the casserole to the oven, uncovered, and cook for a further 15 minutes. Remove the bouquet garni and discard. Taste and adjust the seasoning, if necessary. Serve the casserole with plain rice or fresh vegetables such as broccoli.

COOK'S TIP

Use turkey fillets instead of the chicken, if preferred, and vary the vegetables according to those you have to hand.

Potato, Chicken, & Banana Cakes

Potato cakes are a great favorite, but are usually served plain as a side dish. In this recipe, the potatoes are combined with minced chicken and mashed banana for a fruit-flavored main course.

Serves 4

INGREDIENTS

1 lb mealy potatoes, diced
8 oz minced chicken
1 large banana
2 tbsp all purpose flour
1 tsp lemon juice
1 onion, finely chopped

2 tbsp chopped fresh sage
2 tbsp butter
2 tbsp vegetable oil

^{2}/3 cup light cream
^{2}/3 cup chicken stock
salt and pepper
fresh sage leaves, to garnish

1 Cook the diced potatoes in a saucepan of boiling water for 10 minutes until cooked through. Drain and mash the potatoes until smooth. Stir in the chicken.

2 Mash the banana and add it to the potato with the flour, lemon juice, onion, and half of the chopped sage. Season well and stir the mixture together.

3 Divide the mixture into 8 equal portions. With lightly floured hands, shape each portion into a round patty.

4 Heat the butter and oil in a skillet, add the potato cakes, and cook for 12-15 minutes or until cooked through, turning once. Remove from the skillet and keep warm.

5 Stir the cream and stock into the skillet with the remaining chopped sage. Cook over a low heat for 2-3 minutes.

6 Arrange the potato cakes on a serving plate, garnish with fresh sage leaves, and serve with the cream and sage sauce.

COOK'S TIP

Do not boil the sauce once the cream has been added as it will curdle. Cook it gently over a very low heat.

Potato, Leek, & Chicken Pie

*This pie has an attractive phyllo pie shell that has a ruffled top
made with strips of the pie dough brushed with melted butter.*

Serves 4

INGREDIENTS

8 oz waxy potatoes, cubed
$^1/_4$ cup butter
1 skinned chicken breast fillet, about
   6 oz, cubed
1 leek, sliced

$5^1/_2$ oz chestnut mushrooms, sliced
$^1/_4$ cup all purpose flour
$1^1/_4$ cups milk
1 tbsp Dijon mustard

2 tbsp chopped fresh sage
8 oz phyllo pie dough, thawed if
   frozen
3 tbsp butter, melted
salt and pepper

1 Cook the potato cubes in a
saucepan of boiling water for
5 minutes. Drain and set aside.

2 Melt the butter in a skillet
and cook the chicken cubes
for 5 minutes or until browned all
over.

3 Add the leek and mushrooms
and cook for 3 minutes,
stirring. Stir in the flour and cook
for 1 minute. Gradually add the
milk and bring to a boil. Add the
mustard, chopped sage, and potato

cubes, then leave the mixture to
simmer for 10 minutes.

4 Meanwhile, line a deep pie
dish with half of the sheets of
phyllo pie dough. Spoon the sauce
into the dish and cover with one
sheet of pie dough. Brush the pie
dough with butter and lay another
sheet on top. Brush this sheet with
butter.

5 Cut the remaining pie dough
into strips and fold them on
to the top of the pie to create a

ruffled effect. Brush the strips with
the melted butter and cook in a
preheated oven 350°F for
45 minutes or until golden brown
and crisp. Serve hot.

COOK'S TIP

*If the top of the pie starts to brown
too quickly, cover it with foil
halfway through the cooking time to
allow the pastry base to cook
through without the top burning.*

Indonesian Potato & Chicken Salad

*The spicy peanut dressing served with this salad may be prepared
in advance and left to chill a day before required.*

Serves 4

INGREDIENTS

4 large waxy potatoes, diced
10^1/$_2$ oz fresh pineapple, diced
2 carrots, grated
6 oz beansprouts
1 bunch scallions, sliced

1 large zucchini, cut into matchsticks
3 celery stalks, cut into matchsticks
6 oz unsalted peanuts
2 cooked chicken breast fillets, about
   4^1/$_2$ oz each, sliced

DRESSING:
6 tbsp crunchy peanut butter
6 tbsp olive oil
2 tbsp light soy sauce
1 red chili, chopped
2 tsp sesame oil
4 tsp lime juice

1 Cook the diced potatoes in a saucepan of boiling water for 10 minutes or until tender. Drain and leave to cool.

2 Transfer the cooled potatoes to a salad bowl.

3 Add the pineapple, carrots, beansprouts, scallions, zucchini, celery, peanuts, and sliced chicken to the potatoes. Toss well to mix all the salad ingredients together.

4 To make the dressing, put the peanut butter in a small bowl and gradually whisk in the olive oil and light soy sauce.

5 Stir in the chopped red chili, sesame oil, and lime juice. Mix until well combined.

6 Pour the spicy dressing over the salad and toss lightly to coat all of the ingredients. Serve the salad immediately, garnished with the lime wedges.

COOK'S TIP

Unsweetened canned pineapple may be used in place of the fresh pineapple for convenience. If only sweetened canned pineapple is available, drain it and rinse under cold running water before using.

Index

Boned Chicken with Parmesan 156
Bourguignonne of Chicken 216
Braised Chicken 362
Breast of Chicken with York Ham and Stilton Cheese 158
Brittany Chicken Casserole 204
Broiled Chicken and Vegetable Salad 240
Broiled Chicken Quarters with Warm Aioli 248
Broiled Chicken with Pesto Toasts 250
Broiled Poussin with Lemon and Tarragon 246
Buttered Chicken 336

Cajun Chicken Gumbo 304
Californian Chicken 228
Caribbean Chicken 310
Cheddar Baked Chicken 172
Cheesy Garlic Drummers 66
Chicken and Asparagus Soup 40
Chicken and Cheese Jackets 54
Chicken and Corn Soup 30
Chicken and Herb Fritters 60
Chicken and Leek Soup 34
Chicken and Onions 332
Chicken and Pasta Broth 42
Chicken and Pea Soup 24
Chicken and Plum Casserole 232
Chicken and Rice Casserole 366
Chicken Cajun-Style 258
Chicken Chop Suey 150
Chicken Chow Mein 372
Chicken Consommé 32
Chicken Drumsticks Deep-Fried with Herbs and Spices 334
Chicken in Red Pepper and Almond Sauce 312
Chicken Jalfrezi 342
Chicken Kebabs 280
Chicken Korma 316
Chicken Lady Jayne 116
Chicken Madeira French-Style 182
Chicken Marengo 234
Chicken Mulligatawny Soup 20
Chicken on Crispy Noodles 364
Chicken Pan Bagna 50
Chicken Pepperonata 64
Chicken Rarebit 52
Chicken Risotto alla Milanese 92
Chicken Satay 290
Chicken Skewers with Lemon and Coriander 276
Chicken Skewers with Red Bell Pepper Sauce 272
Chicken Soup with Coriander Dumplings 36
Chicken Stir-Fry with Cumin Seeds and Trio of Peppers 132
Chicken Strips and Dips 82
Chicken Tikka 328
Chicken Tikka Skewers 294
Chicken Tossed in Black Pepper 330
Chicken with a Curried Yogurt Crust 326

Chicken with Baby Onions and Green Peas 224
Chicken with Bell Peppers and Black Bean Sauce 352
Chicken with Creamy Zucchini and Lime Stuffing 154
Chicken with Garden Herbs 242
Chicken with Marmalade Stuffing 164
Chicken with Shallots in Wild Mushroom and Ginger Sauce 210
Chicken with Two Pepper Sauce 106
Chicken with Yellow Bean Sauce 354
Chicken Wonton Soup 38
Chicken, Bell Pepper, and Orange Stir-Fry 122
Chicken, Corn, and Mangetout Sauté 118
Chicken, Guinea Fowl, and Spaghetti Soup 22
Chicken, Spring Green, and Yellow Bean Stir-Fry 130
Chili Chicken 348
Chili Chicken and Corn Meatballs 308
Chili Coconut Chicken 350
Chinese Chicken Rice 368
Coconut Chicken Curry 126
Coronation Chicken 68
Country Chicken Bake 176
Country Chicken Braise with Rosemary Dumplings 212
Country Chicken Hotch-Potch 178
Cream of Chicken and Lemon Soup 12
Cream of Chicken and Orange Soup 14
Cream of Chicken and Tomato Soup 16
Cream of Chicken Soup 10
Cream of Lemon and Chicken Soup with Spaghetti 18
Creamy Chicken and Potato Casserole 376
Crispy Chicken 356
Cumin-Spiced Apricot Chicken 324

Devilled Chicken 114
Dickensian Chicken Broth 46

Egg Noodles with Chicken and Oyster Sauce 374
Elizabethan Chicken 110

Favorite Grilled Chicken 238
Festive Apple Chicken 168
Feta Chicken with Mountain Herbs 166
Fricassée of Chicken in Lime Sauce 218
Fruity Garlic Curried Chicken 314

Garbanzo Bean and Chicken Soup 28
Gardener's Chicken 184
Garlic Chicken Casserole 208
Garlicky Chicken Cushions 100

Ginger Chicken and Corn 278
Golden Chicken Pilauf 320
Golden Chicken Risotto 90
Golden Chicken with Mango and Cranberries 162
Golden Glazed Chicken 94

Harlequin Chicken 108
Honey and Mustard Baked Chicken 174
Honey and Stir-Fried Chicken with Beansprouts 148
Honey Citrus Chicken 192
Hungarian Chicken Goulash 214

Indian Charred Chicken 262
Indonesian Potato and Chicken Salad 382
Italian Chicken Spirals 98

Jamaican Hotch-Potch 180
Jerk Chicken 256

Kashmiri Chicken 322

Lemon Chicken 360

Maryland Chicken Kebabs 282
Mediterranean Chicken Parcels 102
Mediterranean-Style Sunday Roast 186
Mexican Chicken 306
Minty Lime Chicken 254
Mustardy Barbecue Drummers 268

Oaty Chicken Pieces 62
Old English Chicken Stewed in Ale 206
Old English Spicy Chicken Salad 78
Open Chicken Sandwiches 48

Peppered Chicken Stir-Fried with Sugar Snap Peas 136
Poached Breast of Chicken with Whiskey Sauce 112
Pollo Catalan 160
Pot Roast Orange and Sesame Chicken 188
Potato, Chicken, and Banana Cakes 378
Potato, Leek, and Chicken Pie 380
Potted Smoked Chicken 72
Poussin with Dried Fruits 194
Prosciutto -Wrapped Chicken Packets 96
Prosciutto-Wrapped Chicken 298

Quick Chicken Bake 84

Regal Chicken with Cashew Nut Stuffing 318
Rich Mediterranean Chicken Casserole 202
Roast Chicken Breasts with Bacon Triangles 198
Roast Chicken in Wild Mushroom Sauce 200

Roast Chicken with Coriander and Garlic 196
Rustic Chicken and Orange Pot 226

Sage Chicken and Rice 230
Savory Chicken Sausages 88
Sesame Chicken Brochettes with Cranberry Sauce 286
Skewered Chicken Spirals 270
Skewered Chicken with Bramble Sauce 284
Skewered Spicy Tomato Chicken 274
Solomongundy 70
Spanish Chicken with Prawns 300
Spatchcock Baby Chicken with Garlic and Herbs 244
Speedy Peanut Pan-Fry 120
Spiced Chicken Casserole 220
Spicy Chicken Livers with Pak Choi 58
Spicy Chicken Tortillas 302
Spicy Peanut Chicken 358
Spicy Roast Chicken 340
Spicy Sesame Chicken 260
Springtime Roast Chicken 190
Steamed Chicken and Spring Vegetable Packets 104
Sticky Chicken Drumsticks 264
Stir-Fried Chicken with Cashew Nuts and Yellow Bean Sauce 138
Stir-Fried Chicken with Chili and Crispy Basil 124
Stir-Fried Chicken with Cumin Seeds and Aubergine 140
Stir-Fried Chicken with Lemon and Sesame Seeds 146
Stir-Fried Garlic Chicken with Coriander and Lime 128
Stir-Fried Ginger Chicken 142
Stir-Fried Onion Rice with Five-Spice Chicken 370
Suprême of Chicken with Black Cherries 222
Supreme of Chicken with Pear and Blue Cheese Salad 74
Sweet and Sour Chicken with Mango 144
Sweet and Sour Drumsticks 266
Sweet Maple Chicken 252

Tandoori-Style Chicken 338
Teppanyaki 344
Thai Chicken Noodle Soup 44
Thai Red Chicken with Cherry Tomatoes 134
Thai Stir-Fried Chicken with Vegetables 346
Thai-Style Chicken Skewers 292
Tom's Chicken Soup 26
Tom's Toad in the Hole 86
Tropical Chicken Skewers 288
Tuscan Chicken Livers on Toast 56

Waldorf Summer Chicken Salad 76
Whiskey Roast Chicken 170